THE *Stunt* KITE BOOK

by Alison Fujino
and Benjamin Ruhe

Running Press
Philadelphia, Pennsylvania

Canadian representatives: General Publishing Co., Ltd., 30 Lesmill Road, Don Mills, Ontario M3B 2T6.
International representatives: Worldwide Media Services, Inc., 115 East Twenty-third Street, New York, New York 10010.

9 8 7 6 5 4 3 2
Digit on the right indicates the number of this printing.

Library of Congress Cataloging-in-Publication Data
Fujino, Alison.
    The stunt kite book / by Alison Fujino and Benjamin Ruhe.
        p.   cm.
    Includes index.
    Bibliography: p.
    ISBN 0–89471–697–2 (pbk.): $9.95
    ISBN 0–89471–713–8 (pkg.)
    1. Kites.   I. Ruhe, Benjamin, 1928–   . II. Title.
TL759.F85   1989
629.133′32—dc 19

Cover design by Toby Schmidt.
Interior illustrations by Bruce Lohr and Liz Vodges.
Typography by Commcor Communications Corporation, Philadelphia, Pennsylvania.
Printed by Command Web, Secaucus, New Jersey.

Photographs—André Baget: front cover, middle (Peter Powell kites), and right (Spin-Offs); pp. 10, 19, 31, 38, 46, 53, 62, 70, 77, 81. Will Brown: front cover, upper left inset (Gellert Zeta Wing); back cover, upper right (Gellert Zeta Wing) and upper left. *American Kite Magazine:* pp. 5, 43, 60, 68. Mary Ames: p. 29. Ken Conrad: 110. Valentine Deale: pp. 20, 73 (lower left), 74, 80. Alison M. Fujino: pp. 13, 22, 47, 49, 50, 54, 56, 78, 110. Francis Hall: pp. 12 (right), 65. Thomas Hollingsworth: pp. 26, 42, 44 (right). Kite Fantasy: p. 14. Kite Festival International: p. 52. Neos Omega: p. 67. Peter Powell Kites: pp. 3, 11 (lower left), 37, 93. Skynasaur Kites: p. 12 (lower left). Smithsonian Institution: p. 16. *Stunt Kite Quarterly:* pp. 9, 23, 24 (top and bottom), 44 (lower left), 45, 51, 73 (top and bottom), 75, 76. Trlby Kites: p. 11 (upper right).

This book may be ordered by mail from the publisher.
Please include $2.50 for postage and handling for each copy.
But try your bookstore first!
Running Press Book Publishers
125 South Twenty-second Street
Philadelphia, Pennsylvania 19103

Before you fly a stunt kite, learn the safety rules on page 25 of this book.

Keep your kite in good repair, and always fly responsibly.

The authors and publishers are not responsible for accidents or injuries resulting from the use of any stunt kite or from the use of the information in this book.

DEDICATION

In memory of David Checkley and Steven Edson Miller.

With thanks to Lawrence and Stuart Teacher, Tom Casselman, Dorothea Checkley, Kathy Goodwind, Daniel Prentice, Ron Reich, Cris H. Batdorff, and Val Deale.

Contents

Preface

I was introduced to stunt kites in the spring of 1988 on the salt flats outside of Weifang, in Northeast China.

Traveling companions Tom Casselman and Scott Skinner had brought along stunt kites.

"I'm going to show you something you can fly, " Tom told me.

As I watched him maneuver this kite in the Chinese skies my eyes got as big as saucers. Running out of patience, I was finally handed the controls and given instructions. I felt a jolt pull from my hands through my arms and into the center of my body. I moved forward 10 feet.

With Tom flying another kite, I was soon able to follow his flying loops and turns. It was simple, visual, and *physical.*

Upon my return to the United States, I called my lifelong friend, Ben Ruhe. He asked me, "How was China?" I answered, "I have one thing to say to you Benjamin: *stunt kites!*"

Many minds and spirits helped to make this book. To all the tens of hundreds of fliers who let us into their airspace, we give our wholehearted thanks and appreciation.

This book can only begin to describe the fun and adventure of stunt kite flying. So read this book, drop everything, and get into the wind!

—Alison Fujino

Introduction

Remember when kite flying was a sedentary sport? You rigged the kite, launched it, coaxed it into stable flight, then stood at ease and flew. Two minutes went by, then five, then ten. Nothing else to do but reach for the picnic lunch.

No longer!

Now there are dual-line stunt kites to fly for real action. They swoop, climb, dive, loop, hedgehop at high speed and with great precision, ripping the air as they trace sky arabesques. Made of tough, space-age materials, these rugged new kites mean continuous action and a great physical workout.

Fliers shuffle and sidestep, lean and bend against the heavy pull, shadowbox with their lines, and sing along with the taped music plugged into their ears.

Flying is aerobic exercise and aerial ballet, fun to do, fun to watch.

Move over Frisbee!

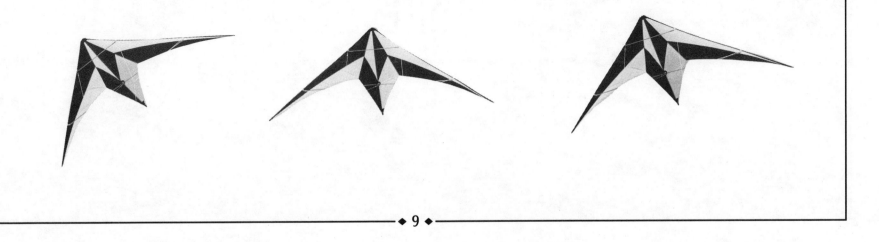

CHAPTER

1

YOUR
FIRST
STUNT
KITE

"The intrinsic quality of kite flying is nature. It's the whole setting, not just the air above you. In a park beside the sea, you have beauty, light, the smell of the ocean. It's a microcosm of what the world is—land, air, water; and you're in the middle of it."

—Tom Casselman, Newport, RI

For a beginner there's a large, confusing choice of dual-line kites. No matter what its speed or strength of pull, any stunt kite can be flown with practice by the beginner. Some, though, are much easier to learn on because they move more slowly in the air and give more time to react and correct mistakes.

Manufacturers understand that stunt kites will be crashed in the learning process, so they make them rugged. The slower-flying ones may be better for a beginner because they crash with less force. Stunt kites *can* be broken, but don't worry. Repairing them is usually fairly easy to do.

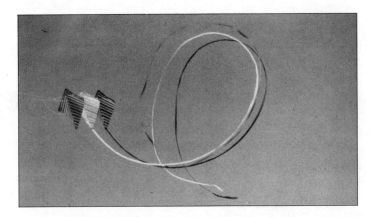

Swirling tails trace the flight patterns of a train of Trlby stunt kites.

Solid Starts

What's the best starter kite? A big, sturdy, diamond-shaped model, like the Peter Powell Stunter, and the Trlby (pronounced "TRILL-bee"), the Spectra Star Diamond, and the Stuntmaster from Dynakite.

The Powell is a good example of a starting model. It has a four-foot-high fiberglass frame, ripstop nylon sails, and a 100-foot tubular polyethylene tail. In flight, the tail swirls around the sky, so you can see where the kite has been. Easy to launch, fly, control, land, and re-launch, the Powell is a smooth, graceful flier. Because of its sturdy space-age materials, it can take a lot of wear and tear.

The Trlby is 36 inches high and weighs three ounces. Its frame is fiberglass and its sail is made of high-density polyethylene. It has a 45-foot tail.

The kite conveniently snaps together. This relatively slow flier is quite durable. For greatest effect, the Trlby is often flown in a train, or stack, of three or more kites, rather like a venetian blind. In the air, the multicolored sails and multiple tails create poetic skywriting. A train pulls harder than a single, but it's just as easy to fly. However, trains are a little more difficult to set up, to launch, and to untangle when they crash. A three-pack Trlby is a reasonable option for a beginner.

Another easy, slow flier is the Skynasaur Skyfoil C26, a 20 x 26-inch stickless parafoil. This completely limp kite is a direct descendant of aerospace research. Inflation is achieved by the rush of air into cellular pockets sewn underneath the horizontal wing. The Skyfoil attains stability from three keels, one on each edge and one in the middle. These triangular fins keep their shape by a system of shroud lines—basically a multi-legged bridle—from which the parafoil is flown. This kite has two great virtues: complete safety because it's soft, and ultimate

Air-filled pockets inflate this Skyfoil C26.

portability because it folds into a lightweight packet.

Fast Starts

Two other types of kites often are flown as beginner models by strong, athletic people eager for big-time thrills right from the start. These two—the Flexifoil and the delta—fly much faster. They also require more strength and better coordination than the Powell, the Trlby, and others mentioned earlier.

The Flexifoil, designed by Ray Merry and Andrew Jones, is a tail-less kite that's completely soft except for a fiberglass spar stretching the length of the leading edge. This kite has cellular pockets that fill with air in flight and provide lift.

The Flexifoil (short for flexible airfoil) looks like a flying beach mattress but develops enormous pull in a fresh breeze. "Your arms getting any longer?" is a favorite jibe among fliers.

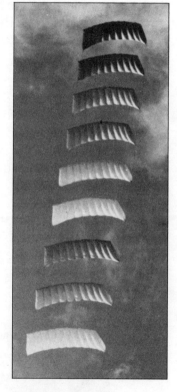

A stack of Flexifoils creates a stairway into the clouds.

An extremely fast flier, the Flexifoil has been clocked at a phenomenal 108 mph.

The best Flexi to start with is the six-foot-wide standard. While fairly expensive, under normal flying conditions the kite should last for years, since it's quite resistant to damage from crashes. Because the design is patented, the Flexifoil has no imitators.

The kite that creates the most excitement is the tail-less "big wing" delta that rips and roars through the sky with precision, beauty and drama. The delta shape has popularized team formation flying and helped establish festivals exclusively for stunt flying. Based on the design of the famous Rogallo flexible wing, which made hang gliding so popular, deltas usually have ripstop nylon wings, tubular fiberglass frames, and are often flown with thin, extremely tough, low-stretch line such as Kevlar.

The delta has an exceptionally taut trailing edge that vibrates in flight and causes the kite to buzz like a jet. You can't miss a delta—its whining noise draws attention to the kite and its flier. First-time viewers sometimes ask, "Where's the motor?"

The delta style is probably the most widely copied of all maneuverables. Excellent examples are the Hawaiian Team Kite, which launched the whole precision flying movement, and its brother, the faster Spin-Off.

Other excellent "big wings"—with wing-spreads of some eight feet—are the Spyrojet

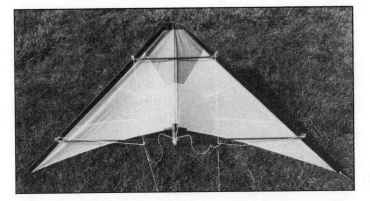

Big-wing deltas such as this Spin-Off sound like airplane engines when flown.

(from Canada), Swept Wing, 2200CC, Spectrum Dart, Peter Powell Wing, Avenger, NoNaMe, Star Dart, Super Sky Dart, Phoenix, and Renegade, among others. These kites are expensive: $100 or more for the kite and the high-tech line. But they are the first choice of many. They're also rugged and will buck a lot of wind, but be prepared for a battle.

Challenges

Once you're doing well with your first kite you can challenge yourself in a number of ways.

One is to learn to fly increasingly difficult and precise aerial maneuvers (see Chapter 3).

Another is to "train" or "stack" your kite with more of the same model until you get a stump-puller of a combination. Stacks require more strength and skill in handling—especially in a high wind that increases their pull.

Because of its small sail area, the Hyperkite Cruiser, for more advanced fliers, is wonderful for stacking. Jacob's ladder trains of 30 or more can be flown to great effect. With their tails swirling and curling, such an ensemble paints a lovely aerial ballet of color and movement.

Robert Loera, of Honolulu, HI, flies a seemingly infinite train of Hyperkites.

Experienced fliers may want to try ultra-light versions of some popular models. These challenge the flier to deal with winds as low as three mph, and the ability to fly under such difficult conditions provides a lot of pleasure to some fliers. Ultra-lights are good for parts of the country where winds are typically quite light. Keep in mind that because these kites are more delicate in construction, they are more breakable.

CARING FOR YOUR KITE

Stunt kites are relatively indestructible, and many fliers report logging upwards of 500 hours' flying time with a favorite kite with no problems at all. Here are some suggestions to help you keep your kite in good condition.

○Avoid diving your kite onto a parking lot, yanking it out of a tree, or crashing it into heavy surf where the weight of the water will mangle it.

○A minor rip in a sail can be repaired with ripstop nylon tape. A larger tear can be repaired by sewing on a patch. If a tear is too large to patch, you'll have to buy a new sail (but that's cheaper than buying a new kite). *continued*

○ If a nosepiece or strut becomes damaged, a replacement may be available from the store that supplied the kite. (When you replace struts and other parts, be sure your repair job maintains the kite's symmetry and balance.)

○ Limit your kite's exposure to the sun. Flying it is one thing, but staking it out in the field for hours and hours so that others can admire it leads to serious ultraviolet-ray damage to the sail. Sunlight weakens the fibers of ripstop nylon and fades your kite's bright colors.

○ Kite line also suffers from unnecessary exposure to ultraviolet rays. Expensive Kevlar line is particularly vulnerable.

○ Don't let flying lines become badly worn. Avoid stepping on your lines, or dragging them across a parking lot or any other especially abrasive surface.

Carrying and Storing

Since most kites are sold with a nylon sheath case, transporting kites is no problem.

○ If you have several kites to tote, consider acquiring a strong cardboard tube to bundle them in, keeping each kite separately wrapped.

If you want a carrying case that's extremely strong and lightweight, get some PVC (polyvinyl chloride) tubing (used in plumbing) from a hardware store. Cut the tube to an appropriate length, cap it with a piece of cardboard, and maybe even attach a carrying handle. This is one way to guard your kite from the ravages of airline baggage handling if you have to store it in a luggage compartment.

If you want to keep your kite with you in the passenger compartment of a plane, be aware that you'll have to stow it in an overhead compartment that may be no more than 40 inches long.

○ Long-term storage is easy. Since spars are warp-proof, you can hang the kite by the strap of its carrying case, stand it up in a corner, or lay it flat on a shelf as long as it won't get crushed by gear on top of it. The storage area should be cool and dry.

Paul Garber: Grand Patriarch of Flight

Smithsonian historian emeritus Paul Garber has seen the entire history of aeronautics evolve during his lifetime.

As a nine-year-old he saw the Wright brothers demonstrate their military biplane in 1909 ("astonishing—I've never gotten over it"), and soloed as a pilot in 1915 in a self-made, 20-foot glider. Garber solicited and took personal delivery of the "Spirit of St. Louis" from Lindbergh on behalf of the Smithsonian Institution. He also acquired for the Smithsonian the Wrights' "Kitty Hawk Flyer," the first powered and controlled aircraft.

A Smithsonian staff member since 1920, Garber has served in a variety of important positions, including curator. When it came time to build the giant National Air and Space Museum in Washington, D.C., there were no worries about filling it to the brim with the most significant aircraft and aeronautical memorabilia—Garber had been systematically collecting them for the government. Amid all the honors bestowed upon him, Garber cherishes one above all: The National Air and Space Museum's enormous conservation facility in suburban Silver Hill, MD., is named after him.

As an aircraft recognition officer in the U.S. Navy during World War II, Garber invented a dual-line kite (the Navy Target Kite, or NTK). (See an illustration of the NTK on page 41.)

While aboard the carrier *Block Island* in 1942, Garber saw gunners on his ship practice-firing at balloons and clouds. This made no sense to Garber, who had been flying kites since the age of five, and who had written a manual on the subject for the Boy Scouts in 1931. He promptly made a traditional single-line kite and watched as the gunners happily blasted away at it. However, Garber thought he could do much better.

Planning at night and experimenting by day, he came up with a better kite: "A simple three-stick barn kite," in his words, that he equipped with two lines and a rudder for maneuverability. No tail was needed.

The kite was flown with a wooden reel mounted on a bar with flying lines which led to the kite though a bridle stick. The kite had 15 square feet of surface, required a 12-mph breeze to fly (no problem aboard a moving ship), and would fly at twice the speed of the wind, even faster when diving.

Garber painted a silhouette of an enemy plane on the kite's fabric cover. To the gunner, the target kite at 200 yards looked about the same size as a fighter plane a quarter-mile away.

The kite could dive, loop, and bank sharply. It plummeted like a stricken airplane hurtling earthward with its engine at full power. It could recover with all the ease of a pilot hauling back on his stick and racing for altitude.

Garber arranged to demonstrate his invention to Captain Luis de Florez, chief of the Navy's special devices division, on a downtown Washington rooftop. De Florez said, "That's the best darned kite I've ever seen. Make me six more—today."

At the Navy's old sail loft, Garber scrounged enough material and sewing help to deliver the kites by nightfall. An order for another six followed, then 50, then 100, and after general military approval was gained, mass production soon began. Eventually, more than 300,000 of the kites were produced and shipped in boxes of 25 to American military units worldwide. The Navy even took out a patent on the NTK in Garber's name.

After the war, the kites surfaced here and there as military surplus, but few now remain.

The Smithsonian has one in its kite collection, courtesy of the inventor. Another was auctioned at a recent kite event for $600.

Although he is officially retired, Garber still goes to work daily at the National Air and Space Museum, where he answers phone calls, chats with visitors, and, with volunteer secretarial help, copes with mounds of personal mail. By design his office is closest to the library. "With his amazing recall for aeronautical history, we consider him an adjunct of the library," says a museum official.

A round man with disarming charm and shocks of gray hair, Garber speaks, sage-like, from the desk chair in his office.

His major project now is writing his "aerobiography" ("I'm not much for autos," he jokes). A great deal of information about the many important aircraft he has acquired during the course of his Smithsonian career is filed away in his head, and he is trying to put everything down on paper.

His office is filled with airplane pictures, memorabilia, and general aeronautical clutter. He even has an airplane on his tie. Hanging from the ceiling of his office are two original tetrahedral kite frames used by an early neighbor of Garber's,

Alexander Graham Bell. The kite frames are a reminder that amid all the glamorous aircraft in the museum, Garber loves kites with a special passion. He has run the Smithsonian's kite festival for two decades and knows all about stunters.

Talk about kites gets Garber to reminiscing about a kite built by the Wright brothers.

"Before then," he says, "kites were controlled on two axes—yaw and pitch. *Their* kite also controlled roll. It was one of the most important vehicles ever built."

It's no surprise that a mind steeped in the Wrights would be full of ideas like the one that led to the development of the NTK. As a friend comments, "Garber's full of the Wright stuff."

CHAPTER

2

TIME
TO FLY

"Flying a stunt kite is magic. You're up there with the kite. There's nothing else around you. You feel every puff of the wind. It's the closest thing you can get to flying with your feet on the ground."

—Don Tabor, San Diego, CA

Flying a high-tech stunt kite is easy.

The kite is flown with two lines, one attached to each side of the front of the kite. Pull right, the kite goes right; pull left, the kite goes left. Keep your hands together, and the kite flies straight in the direction it's pointed.

By a combination of right and left pulls, you can make the kite do maneuvers: loops, figure eights, power climbs, high-speed dives, ground sweeps, and lots more.

That's basically all there is to it.

"If you can make a kite do a three o'clock pass and a nine o'clock pass and a loop either way, you've got it," says champion flier Malcolm Moore. "It takes 15 minutes to learn."

Well, an hour or so for most people, anyway. But if you're reasonably well-coordinated, you should have no trouble becoming adept. And you'll have fun from the start. For spontaneous appeal, stunt kite flying is hard to beat.

Wind

Before you head for the field, check the wind requirement for your kite. Stunt kites tend to need more breeze than the single-line kites you may remember from your childhood. Phone the weather bureau for a wind reading and forecast.

In general, a novice should have winds in the 12 to 20 mph range; 15 mph is ideal. Beyond 25 mph, it's probably smart to hold off until the winds decrease a bit. (To calculate wind speed yourself, see page 28.)

Helpful Tools

Take along a pocketknife or a screwdriver. This will be useful in case you have to pry open tight new bridle snaps so that you can thread line into them. You'll also need a wooden or metal stake (a screwdriver works well too) about a foot long to anchor your line handles. (More about how this works later.)

You'll probably need to tie at least one simple knot. Here are three that may come in handy:

The Overhand Loop

This is a slip-proof, fast-connecting knot used to make nooses at the ends of link lines and bridles, and to make small nooses to attach to kite frames.

Take your line, double it over, make a loop and insert the leading end through it.

The Lark's Head (In-line Loop) Knot

For connecting link lines to lead bridles for attaching trains of kites.

Double-loop the noose on the end of the lines. Pull tight. To disconnect, just pull back of double loop. It's very easy and quick.

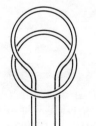 

The Bowline Loop

Used to secure a loop at the end of a line before making other knotting connections to bridles and the kite. Perfect for tying control lines to swivels.

Tie a knot in the end of a line, make a large loop and thread the line as illustrated. Carefully tighten the knot close to the end of the line.

Where to Fly

A stunter needs much more space than a conventional kite—on land as well as in the air. Figure half a football field or a bit more.

You'll need a flat and unobstructed area. If there's no beach or park handy, look for a cutover field or a meadow. Trees and houses break the flow of the wind and cause turbulence, so stay as far away from them as possible. Small hills also cause turbulence. Fly on the upwind side of any obstacle.

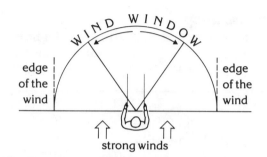

Rules to Fly By

Flying a kite near power lines, pylons, and poles is dangerous and stupid. Another hazard is the highway. Avoid flying a stunt kite near a busy road since it is a major distraction to drivers.

Once you start flying, watch for people walking into your area. The thrill of flying will absorb you, but pay attention. Never, *ever,* fly over the heads of people.

Assembling Your Kite

Most kites are sold completely assembled. All you need to do is to fit the spars into plastic sockets to give the kite shape. This process usually takes only a few minutes and can be done at the flying site.

Read the instructions that come with your kite. They're simple, and they include illustrations. If you follow the instructions, you won't have any trouble getting your kite ready to fly.

Assembling a stunt kite is just a matter of minutes.

Prepare to Launch

Determine wind direction and place the assembled kite on its back with its nose toward the wind. Have a friend help hold the kite down. (For a solo launch, see page 26.)

Connect the ends of the flight lines to the kite's bridles as illustrated in the directions.

Unlike single-line kites that can be launched close to the flier and then flown higher and farther away by paying out line, stunters operate well only when full line length is used from the start. *This means that you must unravel the entire line before the launch.* Not using the entire line at the beginning of flying is the single most common error made by beginners.

Have your friend hold the kite with its back toward him or her and the kite's nose pointed upward. Stepping backward, unravel the lines to their full length exactly upwind of the kite. (As you move backward, the wind should be at your back.) Lay the lines out parallel to each other on the sand or grass a foot or so apart. Be sure there aren't any kinks or other obstructions in the lines. (Line length is normally 100 to 150 feet.)

When you reach the end of the lines, make sure they are exactly the same length. If they are unequal, wrap the longer line around the knob on the kite handle until it matches the length of the other line. You won't be able to control your kite well unless the lines are perfectly equal in length.

Ask a friend to hold your kite as you prepare for launching.

Launch

Make sure there are no people in your flying zone and no obstacles behind you. Check to be sure that the flying lines are untwisted and that the kite is exactly downwind (in the direction toward which the wind is blowing). The wind should be blowing against your back as you face the kite.

Now grasp the handles and raise them chest high. Instruct your friend to raise the kite in the air, with the nose pointing up. Pull slightly or take a step backward to bring the flying lines taut (don't put too much pressure on them or you'll pull the kite right out of your friend's hands).

When you signal a launch, your friend pushes the kite upward and releases it. As you give the command ("Let go!") pull back on the handles and take a step backward. The kite shoots skyward.

Let it go straight up until it's flying almost above you, high in the sky. You'll have noticed that the sharp pull of the kite has eased as the kite climbs. The kite is flying at the edge of the wind above you and offers little resistance to the breeze. It floats back and forth. If it leans to the right, pull on the left handle slightly to correct this; if it leans to the left, pull on the right handle.

Keep the lines of your kite taut.

To launch, pull back on the handles as you take a step backward.

You have put the kite into "neutral," or "parked" it.

Now take a breather and get ready for your first maneuver.

Staying Safe

Stunt kites pose a set of concerns new to the world of kiting.

High-speed kites, ultra-strong lines, and a feeling of complete control may tempt you into showboating over the heads of spectators. Don't take a chance. You must think safety when you fly stunters! It's mandatory, as well as being elemental good manners.

○ Fly in open areas, away from people, trees, buildings, and roads.

○ Know the wind conditions you and your kite can handle.

○ Avoid rocky, obstacle-strewn fields; they can trip you up.

○ Use only equipment that is in good repair.

○ Avoid electric wires.

○ Stop flying when a thunderstorm approaches, or if your flying lines become wet because of extreme humidity or dew.

○ Don't use wire as flying line.

○ Don't lend your equipment, particularly a large stack of kites, to an inexperienced flier.

○ Never fly a hard-pulling kite without wearing gloves, or using handles or wrist straps.

○ Don't leave your kite staked out and unattended. It might take off, fly by itself, and hurt someone.

○ Fly downwind from single-line fliers. They can't maneuver, and usually fly at a higher angle.

○ Gain permission before flying near a stunter already on the field.

○ Think ahead. Plan for that worst-case emergency.

○ At all times, be courteous and use common sense.

Solo Launch

Let's assume you have no help. Most kites can be self-launched fairly easily.

After assembly, place the kite on its back in the sand or grass with its nose pointing toward the wind. Attach the flying lines to the bridle points. Before unraveling the lines, anchor the kite to keep it from blowing away. Put something with some weight on the nose, so the wind can't get under the kite and blow it away. (Use a jacket, or whatever else is handy. If you're at the beach, use handfuls of sand.)

After laying out the full length of the lines upwind and making sure the lines are equal, insert the stake you have brought along through both handles (stack them, one on top of the other).

Retrace your steps downwind to the kite.

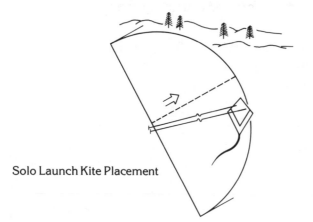

Solo Launch Kite Placement

Remove the weight from the nose and pull the lines taut against the stake. Position the kite for the launch by standing it with its nose upward. (This will prevent the kite from taking off by itself.) Lean the kite backward in the direction the wind is blowing. The tension from the flying lines will hold the kite upright.

A delta-shaped kite is easy to launch because of its triangular shape. The kite can sit upright on its two wing-tips. If you are launching a diamond-shaped kite, angle the kite to one side with its nose in the air.

Return to the handles, take them in your hands, and remove the stake from the ground. Place the stake somewhere safe and out of the way. Raise the handles carefully to chest level. Keep the lines taut; otherwise, the kite will fall over. If you use too much pressure on the lines, the

Use a stake or screwdriver to secure your handles before a solo launch.

kite will launch before you're ready.

Make sure the flying area is clear.

Launch the kite by pulling sharply as you take a step backward. The kite should rocket upward.

Even with practice you may abort a launch. Be prepared to walk back and forth a few times.

If you've pulled off the self-launch, park the kite high in the sky and congratulate yourself. Then get ready for action.

TROUBLESHOOTING

Most kite-flying problems are easily solved. If your kite . . .

o *Nose-dives immediately after launch,*
The lines may be reversed; land the kite and reattach the lines correctly.
A flying line may be caught on a wing-tip; land the kite and disentangle.
You may be over-controlling your kite; restrict your hand movements.
Your kite may not be assembled correctly; land it and make necessary adjustments.

o *Goes left when you pull right, or vice versa,*
The flying lines are reversed; land the kite and reattach the lines.

o *Flutters and offers little pull,*
The bridle is too high; land the kite and move the bridle towclip about ½ inch away from the nose. If the kite still flutters, move the towclip back another ½ inch.

o *Pulls too hard and doesn't climb, or climbs poorly,*
The bridle is too low; land the kite and move the bridle clip toward the nose. (Don't move the clip more than ½ inch at a time.)

o *Handles better on one side than the other,*
Land the kite and make sure the bridle towclips are symmetrical; if not, adjust as necessary.

If your kite is well adjusted but still fails to climb and responds poorly to control movements, the wind may have become too light; land the kite and wait a while, or call it a day.

CALCULATING WIND

The English Admiral Francis Beaufort (1774–1857) devised a scale of wind forces described by name and range of velocity, classified from force 0 to force 12.

While the admiral's rating system for the accurate recording of wind speed was developed for seafarers, it has since been modified for land use and is an excellent aid to wind awareness for stunt kite fliers.

Beaufort Force Number	Miles Per Hour	Wind	What to Look For	When to Fly
0	0–1	calm	smoke rises vertically	not worth flying
1	2–3	light air	smoke drifts slowly	start thinking about it
2	4–7	light breeze	leaves rustle	keep thinking
3	8–12	gentle breeze	small flags fly	use lightweight equipment only
4	13–18	moderate breeze	trees toss, dust flies	ideal flying
5	19–24	fresh breeze	small trees sway	conditions
				particularly favored by experts
6	25–31	strong breeze	large branches sway	you'll get a real physical workout
7	32–38	moderate gale	trees in motion	for experts only
8	39–46	fresh gale	twigs break	danger, don't fly
9	47–54	strong gale	branches break	
10	55–63	whole gale	trees snap	
11	64–72	storm	widespread damage	
12	73–82	hurricane	extreme damage	

Francis Rogallo:
Mating Parachute With Jet

Some years ago, a kite club newsletter reported that it received letters now and then from a member named Francis Rogallo. "Having Fran in our club," the newsletter reported, "is like having Michelangelo join your local artist's club."

Even the briefest review of Rogallo's achievements justifies the comparison. Rogallo developed the ideas for the first flexible-wing hang glider, as well as maneuverable parachutes that allow pinpoint landings, and sophisticated parawings that can accurately control the landing of returning spacecraft.

Rogallo's flexible kite, or Flexikite was commercially marketed after World War II. This kite could be flown with either one or two lines. When flown with two lines it was an early forerunner of the delta-wing stunt kites of today.

Rogallo lives in Kitty Hawk, N.C., the site of the Wright brothers' historic flight of 1903. He chose this location for the same reason the Wrights did: its ocean winds and sand dunes make it a fine place to experiment with kites and gliders.

How did Rogallo come up with his flexible wing?

"For years I pondered how to make collapsible airplane wings like boat sails," he said. "I assumed a mast and boom would be needed. Then I thought maybe it could be done without them.

"In the summer of 1948 I thought about doing something flexible using sticks. At this time I was doing tests on parachutes in a wind tunnel. These tests may have gotten me onto the train of thought of an entirely flexible kite. You put a lot of ideas in the human brain and something eventually pops out of it.

"It's interesting; if you look at nature, there are no completely flexible wings. There are lots of *stiffened* wings. Look at birds and insects. But not entirely flexible wings. To me, the flexible wing is revolutionary."

Rogallo once wrote: "If we could combine the shape of the supersonic airplane with the unbreakable structure of the parachute, we would have a fine kite indeed." His stickless flexikite was just such a mating of parachute with jet. Rogallo and his wife, Gertrude, fashioned it from a piece of printed cotton chintz cut in a roughly triangular shape. Rogallo remembered that paper airplanes with a delta-wing shape flew best for him when he was a boy. Using this form, he successfully tested his new kite in a homemade wind tunnel.

The new 17-inch kite made its first commercial appearance at B. Altman's in New York at Christmas, in 1948. The original sail, made from cotton mesh laminated between sheets of plastic, was later replaced with tougher polyester plastic Mylar.

From the beginning, the flexikite included instructions on how to rig it as a two-line stunter.

"Rigged this way, it was so much fun to fly," Rogallo recalls. "It could do maneuvers—loops, dives, landings, takeoffs. Two of us would do aerial fighting.

"My children and all their friends and the rest of my family had the kites. They did team formation flying, too. My National Aeronautics and Space Administration retirement book has photographic proof of this. One photo shows my brother Vernon, sister-in-law, and their three daughters all flying kites in formation. This would have been 1954." This was the apparent birth of stunt team flying.

When Rogallo filed an application to patent his flexikite he declared that the wings could have various shapes such as rectangles and ellipses. Possible additions to the kite included a tail.

"It should be pointed out," the patent reads, "that reinforcements may consist of hollow plastic tubes which are open at their front ends and closed at their rear ends so as to be inflatable by the incoming air and maintained in shape thereby."

This was the "ram air" principle, thought by many to be a recent concept. The idea was hardly new to Rogallo, who had learned in an aeronautics class in Stanford during the 1930s that some early blimps were stiffened in flight when envelopes inside the hull were inflated with air admitted through vents in the skin.

Rogallo has a basement full of his inventions, including the original flexikite. "I show it to people now and then," he says. "It's in good shape. It will still fly."

Does Rogallo feel that his achievements have won him a place in history? It's a leading question that the inventor deals with deftly: "That depends on the historians." But he adds: "As to the implications of my thinking—we've just started on the possibilities."

CHAPTER

3

BASIC
MANEUVERS

"The first time I picked up the handles of a stunt kite, I was seized by tacho kichi, *kite craziness. And people who are susceptible to its ravages are like the Toad of Toad Hall in* The Wind in the Willows *when he was run over by a motorcar: he realized he had to have one."*
—Laurence Gonzales, Chicago, IL

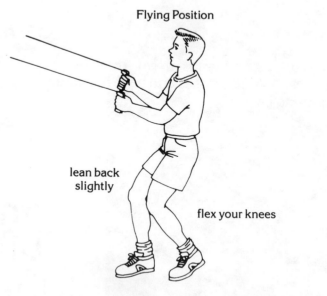

Flying Position

lean back slightly

flex your knees

Your kite is successfully launched and flying around lazily above you. Parked in neutral, it's in equilibrium. Slight movements of your hand controls will keep it in place. Now you're ready to try some maneuvers and have some fun.

This is exhilaration time.

Normal Flight Control

Since the kite is tugging, lean back a bit. Flex your knees a little to cope with gusts of wind that may occur. Some people prefer to fly with feet side-by-side, others with one foot ahead of the other.

Hold your hands side-by-side, vertically, about chest high, elbows flexed. Remember, if you pull with either hand, the kite will go in the direction of the pull.

Opening Maneuver

Pull right to start with. The kite will go right. Return your hand to the side-by-side position and pull left. The kite will swing back to the left.

Repeat this maneuver a few times; then put the kite in neutral and park it.

Now do the same maneuver to the left.

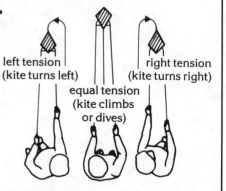

left tension (kite turns left)

equal tension (kite climbs or dives)

right tension (kite turns right)

Fly the kite lazily. The back-and-forth passes should be gentle.

Put the kite back into park. Relax and get your bearings. You've just flown "three o'clock" and "nine o'clock" passes and have mastered something basic.

Try the passes again, but this time link them in flowing swings. Begin to fly a bit more aggressively and work the kite lower and lower. You'll find that these passes easily evolve into ground passes or strafing runs. As you work lower, you'll notice the pull of the kite increasing and the amount of hand movement needed to make the kite respond lessening.

Don't be too bold with the ground passes, or you'll crash. Instead, turn the kite upward and put it back into park. Take another breather.

The ability to put the kite into neutral any time you want is the single most valuable skill you can learn. Practice it a lot.

Ground passes

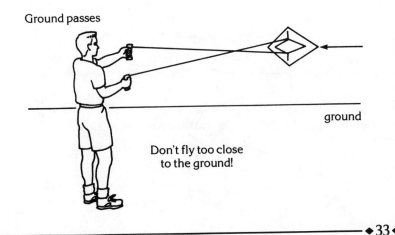

ground

Don't fly too close
to the ground!

Loops

These maneuvers—right- and left-hand loops, or circles— are ones you plunge into.

Perform a simple pull with one hand and hold it. The kite loops around. Anticipating when it will head upward again, instantly return your hand to the side-by-side position and the kite flies straight up to neutral. Do this a few times, then practice looping in the other direction.

Loops and Circles

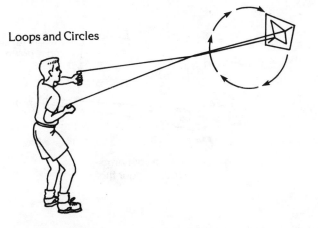

Other Maneuvers

Now that you've mastered the basics, you can experiment to your heart's content. Try flying figure eights (linked loops), double and triple circles, and dives.

Try a Figure Eight

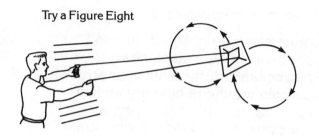

Try a Dive

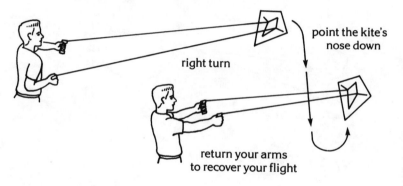

point the kite's nose down

right turn

return your arms to recover your flight

Don't forget:
Crossing your lines means you'll have to uncross them!

Dives are best learned by making the first plunges on the diagonal. Once you have learned how to maneuver your kite in a gentle diagonal dive, you can increase the vertical angle and speed of the plunge.

If you cross your lines by doing, say, three loops in a row, you'll have to uncross them by doing three from the opposite direction.

Landings

At some point, after a half-hour or so, your arms might feel some strain. The trick of landing a kite is to fly it to the right- or left-hand edge of the wind, where the pull decreases, and ease it down for touchdown.

As the kite settles, take a step forward just before it touches the ground. This eases the air pressure on the kite and produces a soft touchdown. As you take the step it helps to extend your arms.

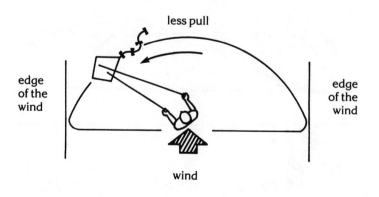

less pull

edge of the wind

edge of the wind

wind

Re-Launch

If you keep the lines taut on your kite as it touches down, the wind will push against the kite's face and keep the kite from falling over. Re-launch it by simply pulling sharply and stepping backward. If this doesn't work, position the kite for re-launch (see page 26).

Crashes

Wind gusts and other unexpected developments may occur in the field of action to make flying a bit more difficult. You may lose control of the kite by reacting incorrectly as you work to get the feel of the controls.

In the beginning, you should expect crashes; the kites are built to be rugged for this reason. Your kite should be able to take repeated smashes without damage.

Of course, don't take advantage of your kite's ability to withstand crashes. One way to ease things for the kite is to step forward anytime the kite threatens to crash—for example, when it's doing a series of fast, uncontrolled spins increasingly close to the ground. Extend your arms as you take the step. This eases air pressure against the kite and lets the kite land much more softly.

Your Flying Progress

After you call it a day and tell your friends what a great discovery you've made with stunt kites (and maybe brag a little about your achievements), you might want to reflect on your first outing.

If you've been able to grasp these two principles of stunt flying, you're on your way to mastery:

○ Your kite will follow your command until you give it another order.

○ Your kite will fly in the direction its nose is pointed when you bring your hands to a side-by-side position.

PERSONAL BEST

After you've gotten the hang of your dual-line stunter, you may want to set some flying goals for yourself. Three months of fairly extensive practice—a summer in the sun—should be enough time to master these skills:

○ Gain capability and confidence in your kite in a variety of wind conditions. This includes learning to adjust the bridle to cope with everything from light to extra-heavy winds.

○ Learn to move on the field to gain more control of the kite. When the kite descends, step forward to make gravity work for you; when the kite climbs, move backward so that your body creates more pull on the kite.

○ Learn the full range of competition maneuvers: smooth launchings and landings, smooth and even figure eights, low and stable ground passes, ground touches with wing-tip, and clean perfect squares (see page 48).

○ Fly a basic team routine with another flier or two.

○ If you have two or more kites, preferably of the same type, fly them in a stack or train to create a more beautiful effect and greater pulling power.

○ Choreograph your own five-minute sky ballet routine to music.

Peter Powell: Stunt Kiting Goes Public

Peter Powell is the man who popularized stunt kite flying.

Early in his career, Powell, an English inventor, developed kites large enough to carry humans. He turned to smaller kites after one of his big ones dropped him 50 feet to the ground.

One day, in the early 1960s, he flew a single-line kite of his own design that leaned annoyingly to one side. Powell corrected this by adding a line on the side opposite the lean so that he could pull the kite upright; for balance he added a line on the other side—that made three lines.

The experiment worked. Powell corrected the lean by tugging the string on the side opposite the one that sagged. When it occurred to him that he could do without the center line, he removed it. This marked the rebirth of the two-line stunter; although others had done it before him, Powell says he didn't know that at the time.

His professional background included creating aerial displays by using inflatables, so Powell thought of adding an inflatable tail to his kite. In flight, the tail wrote its progress through the sky, an innovation that captivated the public. People could see where the kite had been.

Reacting to the growth of the recreation industry, Powell launched his kite commercially in 1972, and it won the British toy of the year award in 1976. Bill Baker, an English engineer, took over the marketing of Powell's kite design in North America in 1980. Using ripstop nylon, graphite spars, and Dacron line, Baker produces the stunter in a variety of sizes, colors, and prices. The design, however, remains basic Powell.

The Peter Powell kite is easy to learn on, forgiving to fly, and can take a lot of punishment. "You can hammer it into the ground time and again and it won't break," says Baker.

A fiftyish bachelor, Powell continues to work on inventions from his home in England, while keeping his business going and showing off his flying abilities in trips around the world.

Out in the field, Powell often flies wearing a three-piece suit, an odd sight at beaches on days when the temperature is in the 90s.

"He's wonderful," says Baker. "He remains the guru."

CHAPTER

4

FROM
SINGLE-
LINE
BEGINNINGS

"I flew a stunt kite over the Civil War battlefield at Gettysburg. It was a little item of peace making a little singing song over one of the bloodiest battlefields in history. We caught a wind from the south; it seemed oddly appropriate."

—Margo Brown, McLean, VA

Take an ancient, subtle, Oriental tradition—kite flying. Add American technical ingenuity, and newly available space-age materials, and you have an exciting new sport. Dual-line stunt kite flying is the beach and park equivalent of windsurfing, and it's easier, cheaper, and more accessible.

Just where did stunting come from? How did it evolve? It's an interesting story.

Traditional single-line kites of every description, from a child's two-stick kite to massive Japanese *rokkakus* requiring dozens of people to launch and fly, have been flown around the globe for many centuries. Few parts of the world are without their own kite traditions. Kites are flown in celebration and for utilitarian purposes. They are poetic and pleasurable.

Early Multiple-Line Kites

Centuries ago, another highly maneuverable

kite was created, the famous single-line Oriental fighter. However, today's two-line controllable kite did not evolve from this kite; the Oriental fighter has a completely different control technique—it's controlled by letting out or taking in line—and its flying philosophy is different (the Oriental kite is an entity, believed to possess a soul; American kites are flown as a reflection of the personalities of their owners).

A Japanese rokkaku kite.

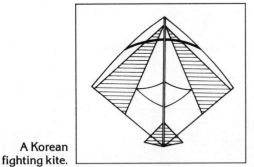

A Korean fighting kite.

In the early 1800s an English schoolteacher, George Pocock, arranged two kites in tandem, controlled by four lines, and hitched them to a carriage. By flying the kites to the left and right of the wind's direction, or tacking, Pocock was able to reach a speed of 20 mph. Pocock called his wind-powered carriage a *char-volant* and patented it in 1826. It was ruled exempt from toll road fees, which applied only to carriages drawn by horse, mule, donkey, or oxen and did not cover a vehicle powered by kites.

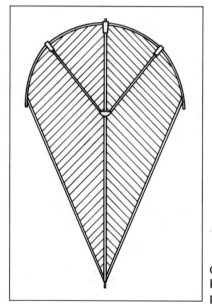

George Pocock's folding kite used in tandem to pull a *char-volant.*

About 1844, a Dr. Colladon in Switzerland experimented with flying double-line kites through a 650-foot arc across the sky. An American, J. Woodbridge David, devised a similar kite in 1894 to carry a rescue line to shore from a disabled ship.

Other records tell of kites flown by two or more lines in the 1800s, when kites were studied extensively for lifting, traction, and other purposes. But when the Wright brothers first successfully flew their airplane at Kitty Hawk in 1903, experimental aeronautical thinking, with a few exceptions, shifted to this wonderful flying machine.

Hugh De Haven of New Canaan, Connecticut, did market a two-line stunt box kite called the air-o-bian in the 1930s, but this kite did not capture public interest.

Paul Garber's Navy Target Kite

Paul Garber, historian emeritus at the Smithsonian Institution, continued the development of the kite during World War II.

Garber had vivid boyhood memories of kites: Alexander Graham Bell, inventor of the telephone and a neighbor of Garber's, had once adjusted a bridle on his kite. As an officer in the Navy in the Second World War, Garber invented a maneuverable kite so that gunners aboard his ship would have a good practice target.

The kite was a standard two-stick diamond, but it was controlled by two lines instead of the usual one. This was the crucial difference. It also had a rudder which was controlled by the flier. Flown from the back of a moving ship, the kite could perform a dazzling array of aerial maneuvers to simulate the flight of an enemy aircraft.

The design of Garber's Navy Target Kite—the NTK—was so successful that it was adopted by the military. In the three years between its invention in the spring of 1942 and the end of the war, 300,000 kites were manufactured and distributed worldwide to U.S. military units.

Garber's NTK was never commercially produced as a recreational toy after the war,

possibly because of its complex flying rig, but today's dual-line stunters, of varying shapes and sizes, owe an obvious debt to it.

The Flexikite

The Flexikite

After World War II, as developments in rocketry opened up the field of astronautics, postwar researchers reconsidered earlier aeronautic ideas.

Francis Rogallo, an aeronautical engineer associated with the U.S. space program, made an important contribution to the development of modern kites with his flexikite, for which he applied for a patent in 1948. Its flexible wings gave this kite lightness, strength, and portability. The delta-wing stunt kite evolved from this kite, which was also the forerunner of the present hang glider.

Rogallo included instructions with his kite on how to rig it as a dual-line stunter.

"Rigged that way," he recalls, "it was so much fun. You could do maneuvers with it—loops, dives, landings, takeoffs. My children and all their friends

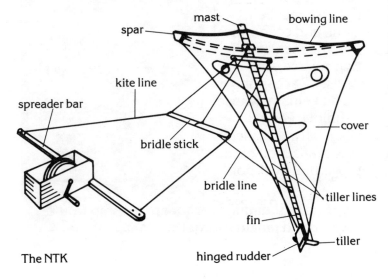

The NTK

had the kites. We even did team formation flying with them."

Forty years later, team-synchronized flying would become a national competition sport.

Today, Rogallo's original flexikite is still available from his daughter, Carol David (see Further Flying, page 83). Her kite is a faithful copy, although it uses six shroud lines instead of the original 14, and Mylar for the sail instead of the original cotton mesh laminated between plastic sheets.

Although his kite never took off commercially, Rogallo's idea of using flexible wings to provide lightness, strength, and portability was developed by the National Aeronautics and Space Administration. Rogallo and NASA worked in wind tunnels at Langley, Virginia, to create sophisticated, flexible wings that filled with air which could be accurately controlled for the landing of space capsules.

Rogallo also developed the limp wing, a variation of the flexible wing that has an unsupported sail area which holds its shape solely through the distribution of air over its surface. The tension from the shroud lines provides balance and support. The lines, in effect, form the kite's stabilizing keel. This kite attains form and lift using pure and efficient concepts.

The Parafoil

Like Rogallo, Domina Jalbert believed that form should follow wind flow, rather than the opposite, as is the case with fixed-wing aircraft.

In the 1960s Jalbert invented a new concept in kite design, the parafoil. Inspired by the wing section of an aeroform balloon he had developed, Jalbert made a fabric kite in the shape of a low-speed wing whose form is created in flight as wind enters vents in its leading edge. Ribs built into the wing maintained the airfoil shape. Stability was added by fins sewn to the bottom of the kite and held in place by a multiple-line bridle.

This principle of "ram-air inflation" made Jalbert's parafoil "the lightest, most efficient, and economical non-mechanized lifting surface ever devised," according to David Pelham, whose definitive *Penguin Book of Kites* called it "the realization of the proverbial sky hook."

Wind enters the pocket vents of a parafoil in flight to give it form.

The Peter Powell Kite

In 1972, Peter Powell, an English tinkerer and inventor, independently created a two-line diamond-shaped kite with an inflatable tail that became the first commercially successful stunter. The tail gave the kite drama: people could see where the kite had been; they could write their names in the sky with it. The kite won the British toy of the year award in 1976.

Soon Powell's kites were being flown all over the world. Well designed, reliable, and reasonably priced, this kite reached the market at an opportune time: outdoor sports, recreation, and exercise for its own sake were becoming increasingly popular.

Bill Baker of Peter Powell Kites shows off a basic Peter Powell stunter.

The Flexifoil

Working on their own at the same time in England were designers Ray Merry and Andrew Jones, who developed a school assignment into the patented Flexifoil (short for flexible airfoil). Although the Flexifoil, placed on the market in 1976, seems closely related to Jalbert's parafoil, Merry and Jones say they had no knowledge of Jalbert's work when they created their design.

The Flexifoil, or "flying beach mattress," is a rectangle of fabric bisected by pockets on its surface that become inflated through a vented leading edge. Its only fixed feature is a fiber spar in the leading edge, which flexes in flight to let the airfoil change shape and adjust to the wind.

When flown in its ten-foot-wide version and in train, the Flexifoil has remarkable pulling power. Flexis were once used to pull a boat at 44 mph, one of the fastest wind traction speeds ever recorded.

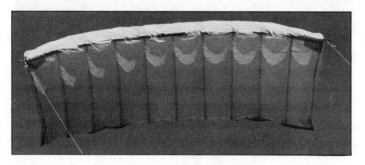

A Flexifoil can exert a pull strong enough to drag a boat across water.

Creations from California

Steve Edeiken from Venice, California, introduced his Rainbow stunt kite in 1977. Although other stunt kites had been flown in train before, normally they were sold as singles. Edeiken sold his in "packs"—three packs, six packs, and twelve packs. This began a profitable trend for sellers. Kites flown in train give new poetry to the sport as their long tails trace arabesques in the sky.

The Rainbow stunt kite (now a collector's item) was once sold in packs of three or more for flying in trains.

Randy Tom, of San Diego, California, expanded the market further with his swift little Hyperkites. San Diego was also the home of Don Tabor, a boat restorer temporarily between jobs, who set out to design a kite that would top anything seen. Aware of space-age materials readily available to make kites and hang gliders—ripstop nylon for sails, fiberglass for spars, and Kevlar for control lines—Tabor came up with a "big wing" delta called the Hawaiian Team Kite. For precision in flying, beauty in the air, and loud crowd-pleasing noise as it flew, this kite set a new standard.

Tournaments

As Tabor had planned, the Hawaiian proved perfect for riveting, Blue Angels-style team formation flying. This development, pioneered by Tabor and friends, set the stage for dual-line kite competitions. Team and individual stunt contests virtually took over many of the kite festivals held across the United States. Today a stunt kite circuit, complete with large cash prizes and touring professional fliers, is close to a reality.

As tournaments blossom, fliers are seeking a competitive edge with techniques such as tethered flying, in which the line is looped through a stake in the ground and the kite doubles back to fly beside the flier. Other skills include "quad-line" flying or the use of four lines for better control, and multiple flying in which one pilot maneuvers up to five kites at once, using ten control lines, creating intricate sky tracery.

Lee Sedgwick, of Erie, PA, demonstrates quad-line flying.

What's Ahead?

With its fast growth in the United States, stunt kiting can be expected to become a popular sport in kite-mad portions of Europe such as Holland and Germany.

In the Orient, where kites have always been culturally important, Chinese kite experts can see a clear link with their great dragon kites, which also can do wonderful acrobatics. At a 1988 kite festival in Weifang, People's Republic of China, the new kites fascinated tens of thousands of onlookers.

Both the mechanics and the spirit of dual-line stunters are easy to grasp and are readily exportable. A surge of interest elsewhere in the world could be next.

CHAPTER

5

TESTING YOUR WINGS IN SOLO COMPETITION

"The lure of kite flying? For some people, it's vicariously being in the sky. For others, it's an exercise in complete concentration, and for others, it's meditation. Some people put on their headphones and listen to their favorite tape or station and have their kites dance to the music in the sky."

—Don Tabor, San Diego, CA

As soon as you get fairly good at stunting, you may want to see how you stack up against others. Kite festivals are a good place to find out. They're educational, fun, and a great excuse for a weekend trip.

Competitions have a number of categories, including novice, so there's no reason to be concerned about making a bad showing. Getting your feet wet is what the novice category is all about.

How can you find out about tournaments?

Kite shops and expert fliers are good sources of information. Each year *Kite Lines*, a quarterly magazine, publishes a comprehensive list of kite festivals in its winter issue. Other kite journals are useful resources as well. The American Kitefliers Association is a clearinghouse of information. Local and regional kite clubs can be helpful. (For addresses, see pages 83–84.)

Once you find a festival that interests you,

contact the sponsor for an advance copy of the rules. This will tell you just what to practice to hone your skills.

Beginning Events

Competition rules are similar at most tournaments. You can compete at a number of skill levels (novice, experienced, open) and in either individual or team events (precision, ballet, innovative).

A beginning flier should probably enter just

Judges evaluate contestants' flying maneuvers.

one competition to start. A good choice is *individual precision*.

Individual precision rules vary from meet to meet, but they generally require you to perform four compulsory maneuvers (one of which may be announced just minutes before the competition begins) and two minutes of maneuvers of your own choosing (freestyle).

Solo Maneuvers

The goal of an individual precision competition is to test technical flying ability.

Typical compulsory maneuvers include the Inward Double Spiral, Square with Inner Circle, Rounded W Power Dive, Inverted Triangle, Square Rigger, Snowman, and Hairpin. The names suggest the figures. Here's what they look like:

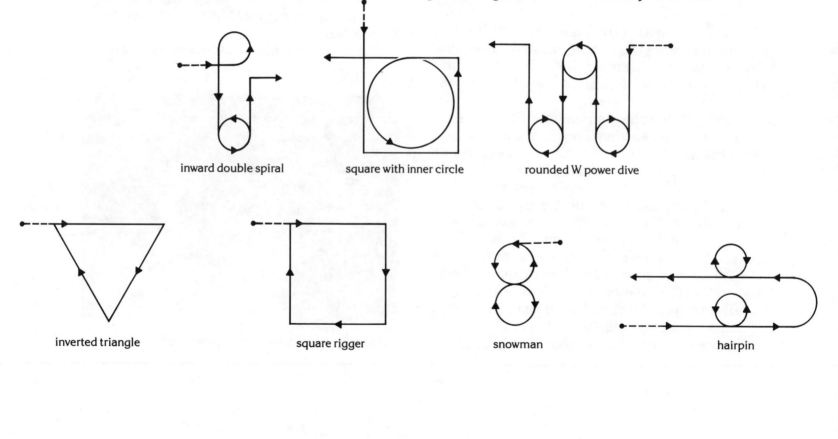

inward double spiral   square with inner circle   rounded W power dive

inverted triangle   square rigger   snowman   hairpin

Scoring Tips

Your score is based on the shape, size, and direction of maneuvers and how closely the figures flown match the ideal figures, taking into account the type of kite you use. Kite speed should remain constant throughout the routine.

You should perform maneuvers in as large an area as possible without overflying the boundaries or touching the ground. Both of these errors result

in penalties. Fliers who make full use of the "wind window" are rewarded by judges.

In the freestyle portion of the routine, the choice of maneuvers is up to the competitor. Maneuvers are judged on the basis of their variety, difficulty, execution, and composition. A good freestyle program has a beginning and a middle that flow smoothly into an ending.

Scoring charts keep a tally of fliers' performances.

Other Events

A really ambitious flier may want to enter more than one event.

In *ballet*, fliers perform a poetic five-minute routine to music of their choice played over a loudspeaker.

In the *innovative* event, virtually anything goes — music, dancing, acrobatics, flying more than one kite, tethered flying, kite switching, use of props such as Frisbees — you name it. The idea is to stretch the imagination (and the number of kites used) to the limit. The routine should hang together, look polished, and be creative.

For an entertaining way to become more involved in the world of stunt kiting, try competition flying.

Creative ballet routines give stunt kite fliers an opportunity to combine music and acrobatics with a variety of stunt kite maneuvers.

Lee Sedgwick and Sue Taft: Adding Imagination

Lee Sedgwick of Erie, PA, represents the new breed that stunt kite flying has attracted to the formerly conservative world of single-line kiting. Enthusiastic and experimental, he has the physical ability and daring to do flying undreamed of just a few years ago.

Tethered flying—"dog stake" flying, he calls it—is one of his competitive innovations. For this maneuver, a dog stake is screwed into the ground and the kite line looped through it to enable the flying kite to double back on its tether. Instead of flying at a distance, the kite glides right beside the flier: it nuzzles, bumps, lands on the open palm. The kite can express a personality.

Tethering is like looking into a mirror: hand movements must be reversed. Instead of having the perspective of looking at the kite, the flier must imagine *being* the kite.

"Quad-line" flying is another Sedgwick invention. Sedgwick uses four lines to control the kite—two for each hand—instead of the usual two lines. Difficult to learn, quad-lining provides greater control of a kite. Sedgwick can casually land a train of kites on the ground and re-launch it as though this were the simplest of maneuvers.

His novel approach to the sport as fun, games, and challenge is catching on with his peers. Don Tabor, guru of team formation flying, says, "Lee is two sandwiches short of a picnic. He's crazy; he's wonderful. He's got me adding emotion to my own flying routines. He has introduced me to a lot of new ideas."

A machinist by trade, Lee finds himself at the beach several times a week to ease tensions by flying. He doesn't practice his competition routines much, preferring to fly for fun. He does ponder and visualize a lot, though. Here's how he put together one prize-winning routine:

"When I want to do a ballet I find a song that makes me want to dance and fly and move around with a kite. When I chose the song 'The Lady in Red' for a ballet by that name, it was because I wanted a love song—I'm in love with my kite— that you could slow-dance to. I must have listened to it a hundred times, getting the feel of it, its tempos and moods. But I rehearsed it only three times before performing. The important thing was the feel of the music. That's what made the performance."

Winner of many championships, including the national singles title in 1986, Sedgwick competes in team flying events with neighbor Sue Taft, also a championship solo flier, whom he trained. Together they captured the 1988 national pairs title. They're so good as a pair they've been called the Fred Astaire and Ginger Rogers of kitedom. Sue says: "We get along so well sometimes we just stand side by side and fly. We don't even have to talk."

As acknowledged stars of the budding national stunt kite circuit, Lee and Sue look forward to international competition. In flying, Sue sees a big advantage to being part of a man-woman team: "It gives balance. People like to see a woman involved. It shows you that you don't have to have big muscles to fly stunt kites."

Lee Sedgwick and Sue Taft, the Fred Astaire and Ginger Rogers of stunt kite flying.

CHAPTER

6

TEAM
FLYING

"People ask me what stunt kiting is. I tell them it's a little like flying with the Blue Angels, except oxygen bottles are optional."

—Laurence Gonzales, Chicago, IL

If you are a competent flier who likes to practice at a beach or field where there are other good fliers, consider organizing a team. Team flying takes stunt kites into a different dimension—and for sheer fun and challenge, it's hard to surpass.

Forming a Team

You can have two, three, or four fliers on a team, but three creates a better effect than two, and it's easier to find three people who can agree on a practice time than four.

Each team member's kite should be of the same type. "Big wing" deltas are the kite of choice for nearly all of the good teams. These kites are extremely precise and make a first-rate appearance in the air. Because they have no tails, they adapt well to close-order acrobatics.

The 1988 San Diego Top of the Line team in flying formation (from the left, Don Tabor, Ron Reich, and Eric Streed).

Positions and Responsibilities

Let's say you have a three-person team.

One of the three becomes the lead flier, No. 1, or captain. A right-handed captain will probably opt to fly on the right; a lefty, on the left.

Since the captain's role demands so many skills, the best qualified person will be obvious. It's the captain who gives the preparatory and execution commands as the team flies, monitors the positions of other team members, watches out for spectators straying within range, adjusts to changing wind conditions, keeps track of wrapped lines and sees to their unwrapping, and deals with emergencies. The captain's kite is flown first and the others follow.

The No. 2 flier stands in the middle, while the No. 3 flier, or wingman, flies on the other side. To present the best-coordinated, most esthetic routine possible, they must follow the leader with accuracy and grace, space their kites well, and speed up or slow down as needed to keep the routine tidy, while at the same time monitoring the field for safety.

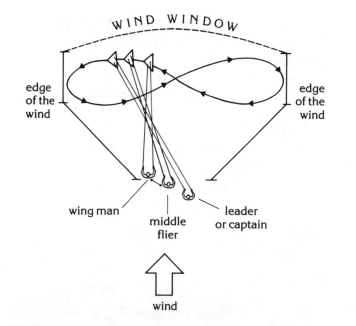

Preparing to Compete

One way a team copes with the demands of close-order formation flying is to use differing lengths of line. The leader's lines usually measure 125 feet, the middleman's lines 120 feet, and the wingman's 115 feet. The fliers keep a distance of about seven feet between one another.

To avoid cutting and chafing as the team's lines wrap and wrap and wrap again while flying maneuvers, team members use the same kind of line. A relatively new line called Spectra is the choice of many teams because it's very slippery—less abrasive than Kevlar, the other line of choice.

Like fighter pilots, team members work out their routines in discussion, by drawing diagrams in the sand or dirt, or by acting out maneuvers with formation flying sticks (three-foot dowels with cardboard triangles tacked on the ends to represent kites).

Captain Stan Mullikin and the Bay Area Precision Flying Team use formation flying sticks to trace their flying maneuvers.

NIGHT SHOW

It's easy to put on a spectacular night show with a stunt kite.

You'll need four-inch Cyalume (also sold as Nightsticks and Lightsticks) capsules. Cyalume is a cold-light chemical widely used in Halloween decorations. It's available in kite, hardware, and novelty stores.

For a delta kite, crack three capsules to activate them and tape one on the top strut and one on each of the bottom two struts. Strapping tape is popular, but any transparent tape works. Make sure to keep the kite balanced.

Most light sticks have a hole at one end, so you can clip the capsules to any of the various kites that have wing-tip swivels. The larger the kite, the more light sticks you can add. (Flying a kite with this added weight may take a bit of getting used to, though.)

Cyalume glows strongly for four to six hours, so you get one night's fun for your money.

Another light source for night extravaganzas are tiny flashing strobe lights. These are powered by inexpensive wristwatch batteries and can be clipped to wing-tip swivels.

Flying Commands

While each team may develop its own commands, many follow the lead of the top precision flying teams and use language familiar to any fighter pilot—"right about," "fall in," and "flank" —to name a few.

Because flying action is so fast, the captain, by agreement, is the only team member who talks while a routine is in progress. The leader delivers commands that develop and maintain a pleasing rhythm.

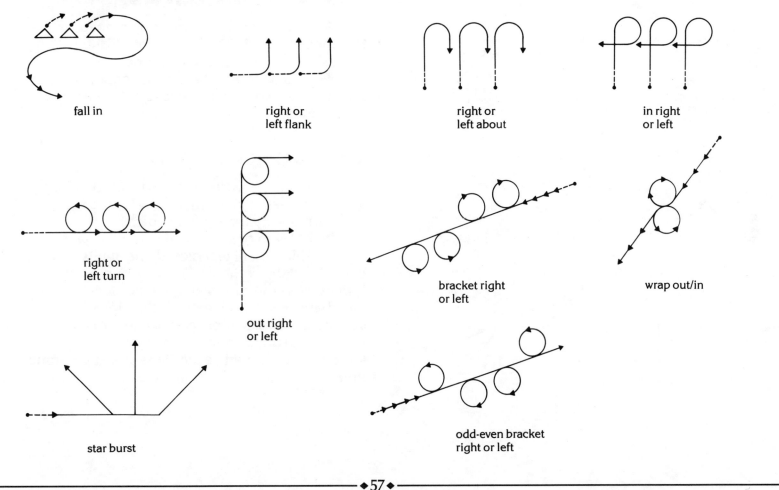

fall in

right or
left flank

right or
left about

in right
or left

right or
left turn

out right
or left

bracket right
or left

wrap out/in

star burst

odd-even bracket
right or left

Basic Team Maneuvers

With this basic vocabulary, a team develops fundamental maneuvers such as these representative samples, developed by the Top of the Line team of San Diego under the captaincy of Ron Reich:

threads

(fliers
pass through
going in opposite
directions)

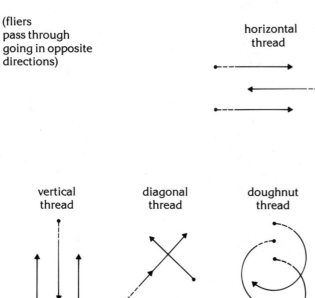

horizontal
thread

vertical
thread

diagonal
thread

doughnut
thread

zipper (out shown in opposite)

peel off

Combining Maneuvers

The team next learns to string maneuvers together. Once this has been accomplished, it's a short step to kite festival competition.

Kite festivals give the team an opportunity to practice teamwork and to measure itself against other squads.

Competing As a Team

The *team precision* event is recommended for novices. *Team ballet* (normally for two fliers), and *team freestyle* are other choices.

In the team precision event, judges want to see an exhibition of technical flying ability. The difficulty of the compulsory maneuvers is not as important as the consistency of each team member in executing them. Judges look for simultaneous execution, performance of mirror images, and uniform speed and spacing between kites. Figures should be the same size at the same time.

A precision team event normally requires a team to perform several compulsory figures (or maneuvers), followed by several minutes of freestyle flying. Typical figures that may be required are illustrated below.

If your team wants to enter precision, ballet, and freestyle flying events, rule books are available from the many stunt kite tournaments now being held across the United States (see page 88).

razzle dazzle (courtesy Top of the Line flying team)

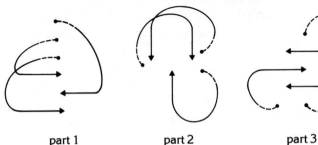

part 1   part 2   part 3

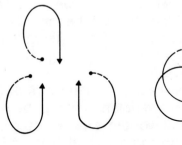

part 4   part 5

team 8's

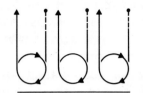

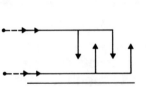   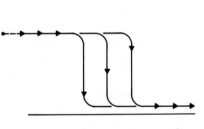

in and out   waterfall

bottom loops

Don Tabor: Father of Team Flying

Don Tabor invented a revolutionary new kite, developed a clever strategy to market it, and now has a booming small business.

As recently as 1982, Tabor, a former pilot, was between jobs and getting around on a bicycle because he couldn't afford a car. Now he has a business in San Diego that employs 30 people, makes 2,000 high-quality kites a month, and is back-ordered. It's a classic rags-to-riches story.

The kite is the Hawaiian, named because it can fly in the wide range of winds found on those islands. Tabor's marketing strategy is simple: fly the kite at as many festivals as possible, and win every prize that can be won. Anyone who sees the kite perform wants one, too.

The Hawaiian Team Kite, to give it its full name, is an eight-foot wide "big wing" delta made of ripstop nylon with tubular fiberglass spars. Tough Kevlar or Spectra are the lines of choice for this kite. All these materials are exceptionally strong and can withstand enormous stress. The kite is not only rugged, but also extremely maneuverable. When it flies in a stiff breeze, it makes a lot of noise and pulls like a horse.

As he hoped, Tabor soon discovered that his kite is perfect for synchronized team flying.

"I always had this idea of team flying," says Tabor. "I used to play cat-and-mouse in the sky with other fliers.

"One day in 1982, at Mission Bay in San Diego, there were six of us flying kites, and space was tight. We decided to play follow-the-leader and had a lot of success doing it. We were elated. We all had adrenalin smiles; our noses hurt, we smiled so much.

"Then someone had the idea we should all make a simple left-hand loop at the same time, and we all did. Screams and cheers! Team flying really does make your heart go pitter-patter. We lived off that for days.

"Pretty soon we tried a maneuver in which even-numbered fliers went left, odd-numbered fliers went right. That worked, too. We could immediately see a thousand possibilities for tricks. That whole summer we worked on pretty simple things, like odd-even turns. We practiced walking together to control air speed. We learned how to deal with wrapped lines. There were other refinements. And everyone could see what was coming—team competitions."

Next spring Tabor did form a team. "Basically," he says, "it was me and the other two guys who showed up most often to practice." Meanwhile, Tabor took his Hawaiian to festivals around the country to show it off.

In 1984, Tabor reorganized his Top of the Line team, with Ron Reich now flying lead on the right, Tabor in the middle, and Eric Streed on the left. The team debuted March 2 at a kite festival in Ocean Beach, WA.

"The wind was up to 40 mph and we got dragged around," recalls Tabor, "but the kite was up to it. My design was a good one. Because the kite is so flexible, air is channeled down the center chute and out. This is why the kite makes so much noise flying."

The team barnstormed the country, and lots of people took notice. By 1985, kite festivals had begun to add team competitions to their formats. Flexifoils with their sweeping turns and Trlbys and Hyperkites flown in trains with long tails were beautiful to watch. But the Hawaiian and its new, swifter clone, the Spin-Off, beat everything in the sky for precision and sheer esthetic appeal, not to mention noise. The Top of the Line team went unbeaten in 1985, 1986, and 1987.

After watching the three fliers in action close-up, one observer said, "They not only move in unison, they breathe in unison."

As team flying becomes more popular and new competitors enter the field, Tabor has the satisfaction of watching the swift progress of the sport he pioneered with his innovative kite.

CHAPTER

7

ORGANIZING YOUR OWN SMALL TOURNAMENT

"Stunt kiting is a great way to make acquaintances. Put a kite up in the air, and within ten minutes you'll have somebody by your side."

—Margo Brown, McLean, VA

Stunt kite flying tends to spread like wildfire on a beach or in a park. One flier gets others interested, and pretty soon a gang of enthusiasts is in action.

It's easy to organize a small tournament of your own. It's great practice for the larger festivals.

Staffing

○ Recruit volunteer help to plan, promote, and staff your tournament. Don't try to do everything yourself.

Scheduling

○ Pick a date, well in advance, when you can predict that the wind will be strong.

○ Reserve a section of beach or a flat, grassy field free of obstructions, measuring at least 150 yards by 150 yards. If you choose a beach, make sure you'll be able to use a large segment of it.

○ Check the insurance requirements of the site's owner or manager.

○ Ask people who are familiar with the wind's patterns to suggest a good hour to start.

○ Make sure you don't conflict with the schedule of another event being held at your location.

○ Choose a postponement date in case a big storm blows in or if there is an unusual calm.

Promoting

○ Advertise your tournament by creating an inexpensive flyer to mail and to post on bulletin boards, trees, and poles. List time, date, location, categories, eligibility, events, prizes, and sponsors. Be sure to list a name and telephone number for further information.

○ Find sponsors to give prizes in return for publicity. Locate big, but inexpensive, trophies for your first-prize individual and team winners, and name both trophies after your principal sponsor or sponsors.

○ Report the date, time, and location of your event to kite organizations and publications for publicity so that as many fliers as possible can attend.

○ Send your flyer to local newspapers, TV and radio stations, and magazines. Try to get an advance newspaper story to bring in more people.

○ If a journalist shows up to do a story, make sure that he or she is given a short lesson in stunt flying to spark interest.

Financing

○ If you need to defray operational costs, consider charging a small registration fee of $5 or $10.

Setting Up

○ Choose events that are easy to run and simple for competitors to grasp. Precision flying and ballet for both individuals and teams should be enough.

○ Be inventive; make up some kite games to play, too. Participants and viewers will appreciate this.

○ Decide on equipment. A portable bullhorn is the single most useful item, since you can use it to control activities at a distance.

○ Rope or plastic tape as well as stakes will be needed to mark off the field.

○ Forms for registration and scoring should be designed in advance. You'll also need a table and chairs for registration and judging.

○ Appoint a tournament director, someone who will not compete.

○ Plan a system to deal with protests. A time limit for filing protests should be established in advance.

Individual Precision Freestyle Score Sheet

Name: _____

Participant No._____

1. Execution	30 points	_____
2. Maneuvers	30 points	_____
3. Composition	20 points	_____
4. Creativity	20 points	_____
Total	100 points	_____

Remarks: _____

_____

_____

_____

Ranking: _____

This score sheet is similar to those used by judges at kite festivals for the Individual Precision Freestyle event.

The *Execution* category measures the ability of the individual to perform the maneuvers.

Maneuvers are judged on their size and difficulty, as well as how closely the individual follows the program format outlined in advance for the judges.

Judges look for smooth transitions between various maneuvers in judging for *Composition*. It is important that the flier link maneuvers in a graceful way consistent with the theme or choreography of the program.

Creativity evaluation is based on the selection of a variety of maneuvers and an innovative sequence of flying them.

The Day of the Tournament

○ The tournament director meets with volunteers and competitors to review rules.

○ Choose a safety officer to keep the events trouble-free and to be responsible for making sure viewers don't wander onto the flying fields, especially children. (The safety officer may be a competitor as long as an alternate is available while the safety officer competes.)

○ Choose judges (in a small tournament participants also may have to act as judges).

○ Set up a table for registration and scorekeeping. Keep good records.

○ Rope off the tournament field. Designate a portion of the space for practice flying.

○ If there are kite sales at the event, decide in advance whether the sponsor gets a small percentage of the sales price to help defray expenses. Also, establish a policy on teaching buyers how to fly. The best policy is not to let novices fly at all until the tournament is over.

○ Hold an awards ceremony on the field at the conclusion of the fly.

Afterward

You may want to hold the awards ceremony at a party celebrating the event at your favorite hangout. In addition to giving awards to the top fliers, try to make an award to everyone who competed as well as to all the volunteers. This encourages good cheer all around.

File the tournament results with the appropriate organizations.

"Flying kites, you can lose yourself in what you're doing. There are no distractions of noise. There's a great connection with your environment. It's a perfect place to escape."

—Tom Casselman, Newport, RI

WHERE IT'S AT:
THE KITE TREE

Where's the single best urban spot in the United States to fly stunt kites?

Kapiolani Park in Honolulu is hard to top. At the foot of Diamond Head, it's dramatically scenic, always warm, and, best of all, home to the northeast trade winds. These breezes blow day and night almost year-round, with an average speed that's perfect for kite flying.

"Hawaii is the best place in the whole country for testing kites," says Robert Loera of Honolulu. "We routinely get winds here so strong they pose a real test to any kite and any flier. The wind is always warm, which is nice. I once flew in a hurricane with winds up to 85 miles per hour, wearing only a tee shirt and shorts, and I was comfortable."

Loera and his kite-flying friends congregate daily at a little park bench and table in Kapiolani across the road from his kite shop, Kite Fantasy, in the New Otani Kaimana Beach Hotel. The group finds shelter from the blazing sun under "The Kite Tree," a 25-foot tree the kiters themselves nourished from a sapling. "We fly our kites within 15 feet of the tree," says Loera.

Who flies? Some people who work nights show up in the morning. Others come in the late afternoon and evening to fly off their tensions from the day's work. Then there are the all-day regulars and the tourists.

"I keep demo kites of all kinds in my shop," says Loera. "Anyone is welcome to take one out and give it a try. There's always an experienced flier on hand to help out with advice."

Loera is king of the field. National stunt kite champion in 1985, he keeps himself in shape for flying by playing two hours of tennis daily. Before turning to kites, Loera was a tennis pro in California where he grew up, son of a professional kitemaker.

Stunt kite competitions are held in Honolulu on a regular basis, and Loera extends an invitation to mainlanders to come out and see for themselves whether or not "the Kite Tree" is a great place to be.

A Revolutionary Stunt Kite

Neos Omega's Revolution I, designed by engineer Joe Hadzicki (center in photo), is a kite shaped like a bow tie. It has a nine-foot horizontal graphite strut to which a line of mesh is attached to spill air. Two sails fly side by side, each supported by a vertical spar.

The kite is controlled by four lines. Weighing just 14 ounces, it has 14 square feet of wing area, making it big but lightweight. It can be flown in gentle winds.

Hadzicki brings the kite screaming downward in a 60-mph power dive, abruptly reverses the controls, and draws it to a sudden halt six inches from the grass. He holds it there for a second or two, motionless, before reversing the controls again and taking the kite straight up and backwards. He can also fly it on a grass-cutting power sweep from left to right, stop it at the edge of the wind, and fly it backwards the way it came. Because the kite spins on its central axis like a propeller, he can make it turn in half the distance of its wingspan.

The kite is simple, different, interesting to watch, and fun to fly. It's novel because it can be controlled not only vertically (yaw) and longitudinally (roll), but also laterally (pitch). (When the Wright brothers figured out how to control these three movements by wing warping, or the ability to bend the wing while in flight, they came up with the first airplane.)

Hadzicki controls his kite not by the usual two-line, steerable push-and-pull hand movements, but by rotating his wrists. His patented curved control handles amplify commands given to the kite.

In the fall of 1988, on the crowded National Mall in Washington, Hadzicki showed his creation to Paul Garber, the Smithsonian curator and kite inventor. "That is indeed wonderful," said Garber. "I'm very impressed. I've never seen such maneuverability coming out of a kite. It's an honor and a privilege for me."

As the ultimate accolade, Garber requested the kite as an addition to the permanent collection of the National Air and Space Museum. Hadzicki, who had studied Garber's World War II patent for the renowned Navy Target Kite, agreed on the spot.

Ray Merry and Andrew Jones: The Flexifoil Partners

The Flexifoil—or "flying mattress," as it's sometimes called—is a bizarre kite with suitably strange beginnings.

Industrial designers Ray Merry (pictured) and Andrew Jones, while working on a joint sculpture project at a college in Newcastle-upon-Tyne, England, explored various wind-inflated shapes and designed one as an airfoil to lift others into the sky. Their first wind-inflated sculpture was made of polyethylene plastic sheeting, repeatedly patched with tape. It eventually flew well, to their surprise, *upside down:* the kite had crashed, flipped over in the wind, and launched itself back into the air. From this first accidental inverted flight emerged the principle that became the basis of their patented design.

The Flexifoil—short for "flexible airfoil"—has evolved from that odd beginning in 1972 to become a renowned dual-line stunter, famed for its sweeping flight, whooshing sound and raw speed. The kite has been clocked at more than 100 mph. When flown in Jacob's-ladder trains, it becomes the workhorse of the sky.

Its exceptional pull has been harnessed to drag humans across beaches (sometimes inadvertently), power dramatic aerial leaps by fliers, pull fliers wearing skis across ice, and tow sailboards and even boats. Adapted as a self-adjusting wing with an undercarriage and small motor, the kite has even evolved into an ultralight aircraft notable for its lack of complicated rigging, its slow speed, its extreme stability, and small pack-down size.

In standard versions with spans of four, six, and ten feet, the rectangular Flexi has ten or more ripstop nylon pockets, or cells, bisecting the kite's surface. These inflate with air through a vented leading edge as the kite moves forward.

The Flexifoil gets its name from the flexing of the single carbon fiber spar in the leading edge. This flexible spar enables the airfoil to change its shape in flight and adjust to winds as light as eight mph and as strong as 50 mph and more.

It was this phenomenon that Merry and Jones observed that day when the kite flipped over and flew itself. They saw that the kite bowed downward at the tips by itself and climbed faster because of this. By eliminating all bridle lines except the ones from the wing-tips, they emphasized the kite's self-flying capability. On today's Flexifoils, a flying line is attached to each end of the leading edge spar and the wind-generated lift forces are transferred from there to the flier's hands. By manipulating the lines, the flier can alter the kite's angle to the wind, and make it turn. Thus the Flexi can be flown acrobatically.

Because of its construction, the kite has a remarkable ability to withstand high-impact crashes. The spar flexes on impact and is almost immune to fracture; the remainder of the kite, being soft, can be injured only by something like barbed wire.

Ray Merry and Andrew Jones say the concept of the Flexifoil was a joint inspiration. "We're frequently asked which of us is the primary inventor of the basic idea, the wind-inflated wing," says Andrew. "It's absolutely impossible to determine. We're a single person as far as the 'foil' goes."

If the inspiration came casually, the working out of the conception took a lot of sweat, many years, and the help of family and friends. Not being avid readers, and being accustomed to working things out for themselves, Merry and Jones didn't learn about Domina Jalbert's parafoil design (see page 42) until much later. "It might have stopped us had we known," says Ray. When they did make the discovery, they decided that apart from the inflation element, the two of them were onto something significantly different. The behavior of the flexing spar which adjusts the angle of flying in varying winds seemed to them novel enough to warrant obtaining a patent.

The Flexifoil was publicly shown for the first time October 10, 1976, at the British Kite Flying Association's festival at Old Warden Aerodrome—a long five years after the original idea.

Merry and Jones maintain a steadfast friendship and working relationship. Jones supervises the Flexifoil business from a European base, while pursuing research and development. Merry now lives in the United States, where he focuses on production and marketing. Both continue to take satisfaction from an invention that many feel is one of the few truly original kites of the 20th century.

CHAPTER

8

FUN AND GAMES

"I have herniated disks in my back. Flying kites builds up the shoulder and back muscles. Keeps the pain away. It's great exercise and it's relaxing. Surprising how well you sleep at night."
—Scott Stewart, San Francisco, CA

After the competitive fires are banked at a kite festival, it's time to play. Here are some of the games concocted by kite enthusiasts. Since these games have no hard and fast rules, you can experiment with any number of exciting variations.

Partners

This game tests the ability of two fliers to pilot one kite. One partner handles the right-hand line, and the other the left-hand line. Side-by-side flying is required. The team flies three required maneuvers and then a short freestyle segment. Each of the four units is worth 25 points. Several teams compete in an order determined by random draw.

The team with the most points wins.

Tail Grab

Invented by Steve Coats of San Diego, this is an American dual-line version of the classic Oriental duel between two fighter kites (see *Glossary*, page 92).

Two identical, or similar, kites with equal-length control lines are used. The kites should have tails of identical length, affixed with easy-to-detach Velcro. (If it's windy, tape coins to the tails so they'll hang straight.) The two pilots fly at the same time from within a circle 25 yards in diameter. The object is to maneuver your stunter so effectively that you detach, or grab, your opponent's tail. Best two of three tail grabs wins.

To select pairs, draw names from a hat. The winner of each round faces a new challenger until a winner emerges.

Team Relay

A group of picnickers flying stunters at Golden Gardens Beach in Seattle recently came up with an impromptu team game that's challenging and competitive.

The object is to knock over three cans (or other targets) placed in front of each team of three fliers. One kite is used per team. The lead flier must knock over the first can, then hand the kite to the second player, who upsets the second can, and then to the third flier for the final can. If the kite grounds, it may be re-launched without penalty; team members may assist.

When teams play in sequence, the fastest time wins. When two teams play simultaneously (more fun by far), the squad that finishes first wins.

Limbo

Invented by Ray Merry, co-inventor of the Flexifoil, this game is the kite version of the renowned Caribbean dance test.

"It looks easy, but is very, very difficult," says Merry.

To play, stretch a line at a height of 12 feet between two poles 175 feet apart (or at least a distance greater than the length of the kite-flying lines used). Position yourself with your back to one of the poles and try to pass the kite under the line, first in one direction, then the other, then back again. Each successful pass wins one point. Each turn is two minutes long and each player gets two turns. If the kite crashes, your turn ends. Ticking the ground or the line with the kite is permitted. The flyer with the most points in two minutes wins.

William Tell

Place an apple or similar object on the head of a display mannequin (borrowed from a friendly store owner). Pilots take turns flying ground passes to try to knock the apple off its perch with either the kite or its line. The kite or line must strike the target cleanly; a glancing blow off the mannequin's head doesn't count. The flier with the most successful hits in a given period of time (say two minutes for each competitor) wins.

William Tell emerged in Chicago as the Godzilla Challenge using an inflatable version of the Japanese sea monster instead of a mannequin.

This game is an excellent test of kite control and patience.

Touch and Go

Place cones (available from sporting goods stores) or garbage cans around a field and tether a balloon floating a banner in the sky. The object is to fly your kite so as to touch each cone; in between touches, the kite must be flown up to touch the banner. Players fly in turn.

The winner is the player who completes the course in the shortest time.

Creative Contests and Feats

In addition to games, creative contests for colorful kites, interesting kite designs, as well as innovative flier costumes take place at some kite festivals. Many fliers customize their kites to resemble anything from fighter planes to cartoon characters.

Demonstrations of strength and daring may take place at festivals as well. Kite jumps and drags for height and distance are performed on beaches where there is soft sand. It is wise to remember however that these games are only for the most experienced fliers under the supervision of other experts who have determined that all safety precautions have been made.

Fliers have fun creating innovative kite designs (above) and costumes (below) using a number of themes.

"Arms getting any longer?" Dennis Kucmerowski of Boca Raton, FL, has fun flying with his extended reach.

Val Deale goes Flexifoil jumping on the dunes at Jockey's Ridge State Park, Nags Head, NC.

DOING A "360"

This feat involves flying your kite in a complete circle, close to the ground.

Impossible? So it seems, yet a number of fliers have pulled off the stunt, including Ken Wright of Annapolis, Maryland.

Here's how it's done. Assume the wind is blowing at four mph. Wheel your stunter in an arc from the far left of the wind, to downwind, to the far right of the wind where it stops getting any help from the breeze. Keep the kite turning, and now the wind is *against* the kite. You can maintain control of the kite only by running backward as fast as possible. You'll have to run at seven mph or more, giving the kite a net lift of three mph. As the kite keeps swinging around, it will re-enter the zone where the wind again becomes helpful, and complete the circle.

If you want a challenge, give this stunt a try. It's a great (if brief) workout.

Ron Reich:
King of the Air

Ron Reich coached three daughters to local and state championships in horseback riding, artistic roller skating, and gymnastics, but he vowed that after they grew up he'd find his own sport and become a national champion to show them how it's done.

After discovering stunt kite flying in 1985, Reich (pronounced Rich) fulfilled his pledge to himself within a year by winning a national championship in individual aerial ballet. He then quickly established himself as the dominant American flier. Now he's thinking of expanding globally, hoping to compete, teach, and organize on an international level.

An oceanic engineer, Ron saw stunters in action for the first time during a walk in his home town of San Diego, California. He sat under a tree and watched spellbound for a half hour, then announced to his wife, "This is something I have to do." Within days he had acquired a kite, and was flying proficiently.

Reich is a natural for the sport: he has great coordination, a precise nature, excellent visual memory, and he's ambidextrous. He's the kind of guy who can pat his own head, sing, rub his belly, and tap-dance at the same time.

An exceptional singles flier, Ron was recruited for team precision flying and landed on the hottest squad of all, Don Tabor's Top of the Line team in San Diego. In deference to Reich's talents, Tabor appointed him the captain and signal caller. ("Although I'm the captain, Tabor is the admiral," says Ron.) Tabor took the middle position and Eric Streed flew No. 3. The team later was expanded with the addition of a fourth flier, Pam Kirk, in the No. 2 spot. Top of the Line soon began to dominate team flying through a mixture of precision, lovely choreography, and sheer competitive determination.

As captain, Reich choreographs all the routines, picks the music, and calls the signals. Here's what he does as the quartet whips through close-order maneuvers:

He (1) flies the lead kite, (2) gives the preparatory command for a maneuver as the kites whiz around the sky, (3) gives the execution command seconds later in perfect tempo, (4) watches his teammates to be sure they're positioned correctly, (5) takes safety precautions and keeps track of any other people who may be on the field,

(6) monitors boundaries so the team won't overfly them and be penalized, (7) keeps track of wind changes and adjusts to them, and (8) keeps the group in perfect synchronization with the music blaring over the loudspeakers—all this while trying to make the overall flight as pleasing as possible to judges and spectators.

"The maneuvers must entertain the crowd," says Reich. "I want the audience to receive an emotional experience from our performance."

For Reich, singles flying is hardly less complex. He pioneered flying two kites simultaneously, guiding them with his hands and with flying lines attached to his belt buckle. Since then he's added a third kite to this routine, steering it with his hips.

But he's still not satisfied. He's now working on flying five kites at once, meaning that he'll have ten flying lines to control. "I've pretty well gotten it down," says Reich. His opponents aren't exactly cheered at this new, potentially prize-winning development.

Among his fans, nobody applauds harder than his three daughters, who are only too glad to admit he has indeed shown them how it's done.

Ron Reich in action.

CHAPTER

9

FLYING RECORDS AND FEATS

"I was on vacation five years ago when I saw a Skynasaur stunt kite being flown. 'What is this?' I asked myself. I stopped the car and bought one. Within five minutes I could keep it off the ground; within an hour I was making low-level passes across the sand and doing everything else with the kite.

"I've still got that kite. It's virtually indestructible. I've got duct tape all over it for repairs, but the thing still flies well."

—Scott Stewart, San Francisco, CA

BELIEVE IT OR NOT!

o Wearing scuba gear, Ron Reich of San Diego assembled a delta stunt kite underwater and then successfully "flew" it for a taping of the "That's Incredible" television program. Reich, an oceanic scientist, calculates that one mph of water current equals 30 mph of wind.

o John Waters of Lincoln City, OR, uses a 330-square-foot sparless parafoil that exerts enormous pull in a stiff breeze to help him make giant leaps down the beach, honking a horn he carries to warn people to get out of the way.

Largest Number of Kites Flown

Mix McGraw successfully flew a 210-foot train of 253 small triangular Hyperkite Fighters for more than five minutes at an Ocean City, MD, kite festival. The kites achieved one complete loop to the right and one loop to the left.

Mix McGraw of San Francisco with his record-breaking train of small triangular Hyperkite Fighters.

Highest Vertical Jump/Farthest Horizontal Jump

Lee Sedgwick of Erie, PA, used heavy-pulling stunters to make a vertical jump of 21 feet and a simultaneous outward leap of 75 feet. He did the stunt on soft sand.

Farthest Kite Drag

Dave Town of Sea Isle City, NJ, used a stack of eight six-foot Flexifoils to drag him 2.7 miles along a wet beach near his home. He interrupted the trip several times to surmount obstacles such as piers. Leaning back in a harness and sliding on the soles of running shoes, Town achieved a speed of 10 mph.

Highest Flight

An American women's climbing team flew a Skynasaur stunt kite from its base camp at 18,000 feet on Mount Everest and made a photograph to prove it. This is believed to be the highest altitude at which a stunter has been flown.

Fastest Kite Speed

Troy Vickstrom clocked a 10-foot Flexifoil kite with 300-pound test Spectra fiber line at a speed of 108 mph at Lincoln City, OR.

Longest Flight

Mike Ives-Karter of Stroud–in–Gloucestershire, England, kept a train of three Ace dual-line kites aloft and stunting through three nights. His consecutive flying time was 67 hours.

Most Stunts Flown in an Hour

Stewart Cohen of Babylon, NY, completed 2,911 figure eights, or 5,822 loops, with a tailless Rainbow stunter in one hour's flying time.

Largest Stunter Flown

Ted Dougherty of Pine Hill, NJ, put a 460-square foot, homemade, sparless, air-inflatable stunter into the air and coaxed six and one-half minutes of flight from it, while looping it once to the right and once to the left.

Steve Edeiken: The Rainbow Legacy

In the mid-1970s, a young carpenter looking for a business opportunity saw the prospect of rewarding commerce from stunt kites.

Steve Edeiken of Venice, CA, designed his own dual-line diamond, the Rainbow, and quickly hit on the idea of flying it in trains for greater visual effect. Onlookers who saw Edeiken's stacks of multicolored kites with their long tails carving the sky into graceful arabesques wanted Rainbows, too. Edeiken obliged with three-packs, six-packs, even 12-packs.

Edeiken is vividly remembered as a handsome, charming man with a great sense of humor by AKA official Rick Kinnaird and his wife Eileen. At the AKA national competition in 1979, Steve inadvertently smacked a six-pack of Rainbows into a portable toilet, startling an unsuspecting occupant who fled the unknown attacker. "It was right out of a Keystone Kops comedy," recalls Rick.

At the AKA championship two years later, Edeiken and Wayne Grau of Los Angeles each flew a train of 25 Rainbows in tandem to such dazzling effect that all activity on the field halted as everyone oohed and aahed at the sight. "It was so moving," says Rick, "there were tears in the eyes of many people."

Two years later, on September 24, 1983, while supervising the launch of a giant parafoil kite at Long Beach, Washington, Edeiken's foot became entangled in the shroud lines and he was lifted aloft as a gust of wind suddenly raised the monster kite into the sky. He was carried about 275 feet into the air, worked his way free, but then was shaken loose by the oscillating kite and fell to his death.

Four days later, he was mourned across the country as friends and admirers flew kites in his honor on the evening of his memorial service. Edeiken was just 30 years old.

"Steve was wonderful, such a gentleman; he really set off stunt kiting," says Eileen. "He inspired so many people with his train flying. He was the foundation of the sport."

FURTHER
FLYING

Kites

Where can you find an assortment of good kites? There are two major sources: kite stores and mail order.

Specialty kite stores can be found throughout the country, mainly in cities and at beaches where the wind is good and space is unobstructed. A scattering of stunt kites can be found at museum and park shops and elsewhere.

Walk into any store handling stunters and you're likely to find an enthusiastic and knowledgeable staff member who can prescribe just the kite to suit your needs and your wallet. At some shops, kite staff will be pleased to take you out flying (by appointment) so you can experience stunt kites for yourself on the field of action. In the summer, stores at crowded beaches typically offer lessons in the evening, after the sand is clear of bathers. City stores often have a favorite park, campus, or field nearby for flying.

If you don't have access to a store, try mail order. Ordering by mail or by telephone is quick and easy. First you need a catalog to examine. A number are available, filled with beautiful photographs and drawings of kites in action. The descriptions of the kites and accessories are usually honest and straightforward, and it should be easy to choose.

You can request free mailouts from companies that advertise in any of the glossy kite magazines now being published (see "Magazines," opposite).

Some kites come equipped with line and control handles; others don't—particularly the expensive models. If not, the catalogs will explain what type and strength of line is appropriate for the kite you are buying. For example, the Spyrojet might require 150-foot lines of 200-pound test strength for optimal effectiveness. Choice of grips is similarly easy; just read the catalogs.

Here are the addresses and phone numbers of some stores that offer good free catalogues:

- *Catch the Wind,* Box 419, Star Route N, Newport, OR 97365. 503/265–6928.

- *High Fly Kite Co.,* Box 2146, Haddonfield, NJ 08033. 609/429–6260.

- *Into the Wind,* 1408 Pearl Street, Boulder, CO 80302. 303/449–5356.

- *The Kite Loft,* Box 511 Boardwalk, Ocean City, MD 21842. 301/289–7855.

- *Kitty Hawk Kites,* Box 340, Route 158 Bypass, Nags Head, NC 27959. 919/441–4124.

○ *Klig's Kites,* Deerfield Plaza, Highway 17, Surfside Beach, SC 29577. 803/238-4787.

The flexikite (Rogallo's original design) is available by mail from his daughter for $7.50 postpaid. Write to Carol David, 3009 Creel Court, Woodbridge, VA 22192.

 Magazines

Three glossy quarterly magazines chronicle the American kite scene. All are available by subscription and can be found at most kite stores.

○ *Stunt Kite Quarterly.* This publication is devoted exclusively to stunt kite flying. The magazine features competition news, personalities, flying techniques, and tips. The editor is Cris Batdorff, a veteran flier. $12 per year. Address: Postal Box 468, Manistee, MI 49660.

○ *American Kite.* Daniel Prentice's quarterly magazine focuses on the U.S. kite scene, with substantial stunt kite coverage. Includes features on personalities of the kite world. $10 per year. Address: 480 Clementina St., San Francisco, CA 94103.

○ *Kite Lines.* Valerie Govig's quarterly addresses "the worldwide kite community" and for many years has served as the journal of record for global kite news. It's well written, accurate and often scholarly. The magazine gives extensive coverage to stunt kiting. $12 per year. Address: P.O. Box 466, Randallstown, MD 21133.

A bimonthly newsletter is available from the American Kitefliers Association as a membership benefit (see "Clubs," page 84). Regional newsletters are issued by a number of clubs; an excellent example of this kind of publication is *Sky Lines* by the Chicagoland Sky Liners Club, available with club membership. For information on a club near you, contact the AKA.

A four-color biannual promotional newsletter is offered free by Peter Powell Kites. Address: 1040 N.E. 43rd Court, Fort Lauderdale, FL 33334.

Books

This book is the first one devoted exclusively to the sport of stunt kite flying. General literature on kites is vast, though, and the books on this list have been chosen because they give a fine overview of the kite world.

- *The Penguin Book of Kites.* David Pelham. New York: Penguin Books, 1976. 228 pages.

- *Kite Flight.* Jack Botermans and Alice Weve. New York: Henry Holt, 1986. 119 pages.

- *Kites: An Historical Survey.* Clive Hart. New York: Praeger and Praeger, 1982. 210 pages.

Al Hargus III has written a booklet on stunt kiting that provides troubleshooting advice to the flier in the field. Brief and to the point, the six-page publication is called *The Easy "No Secrets" Handbook for Dual Line Stunt Kites* and is available free from Al Hargus III, 4705 W. Byron Ave., Chicago, IL 60641.

Another booklet is *High Performance Stunt Kites* by Hoy Quan. This 26-page booklet, which is also partly a sales catalog, is available free from the author. Send inquiries to 891 Ashiya Street, Montebello, CA 90640.

An historical curiosity is the U.S. government manual issued in conjunction with Paul Garber's famous Navy Target Kite of 1942–5. Written by Garber, then a Navy officer, the volume (now out of print) was issued by the United States Bureau of Aeronautics and titled *"Target Kites."* You can view a copy in the Smithsonian's National Air and Space Museum Library in Washington, DC.

Clubs

The American Kitefliers Association is a wonderful source of information on kite flying, including stunt flying.

An annual membership brings many benefits: a bimonthly newsletter, kite plans, news of chapter activities, a membership discount at kite stores, assistance in forming a chapter, guidance on educational programs, and technical assistance from experts on request. Liability insurance is available to chapters for AKA-sponsored events. Address: The American Kitefliers Association, 1559 Rockville Pike, Rockville, MD 20852.

Local clubs that devote themselves exclusively to stunt flying include the Skyliners Kite Club, Chicago; the First Ever Stunt Kite League, Grand Haven, MI; and the Surfside Flyers Club, Surfside Beach, TX.

For information on stunt clubs in your region, contact the AKA.

Videos

One way to improve your technique is to watch experts fly. An easy way to see the best in action is with a video cassette such as those sold by the American Kitefliers Association. Professionally filmed at annual conventions, the videos have substantial footage on stunt kiting. Contact the AKA at 1559 Rockville Pike, Rockville, MD 20852.

High Fly Kite Company sells videos filmed at the annual Wildwood, NJ, fly-in. (Footage includes scenes of champion flier Ron Reich assembling and flying a delta stunter under water!) Address: Fran Gramkowski, 30 West End Avenue, Haddonfield, NJ 08033.

Peter Powell Kites sells a sales promotional cassette exclusively on stunters. Address: Bill Baker, 1040 N.E. 43rd Court, Fort Lauderdale, FL 33334.

Several other major kite distributors have produced promotional videos and may have copies for sale. Check kite magazines for advertisements by these firms, and write or telephone them to inquire.

Good Places to Fly

○ *Glamis Sand Dunes, CA*
Ron Romero, Jr., Santa Barbara kite enthusiast: "The dunes run more than 100 miles all the way to the Arizona border. You can only get around them in an off-road motorcycle or sand buggy. Winds blow at 25 mph or more pretty much the year-around. The dunes look like frozen waves. Because there is a small danger of getting lost or stuck, flying there has a certain edge."

○ *Laguna Beach, CA*
The beach in front of the Ritz-Carlton Hotel. Eric Streed, member of the Top of the Line precision flying team: "You fly in a cove which is just gorgeous. The water is an ice-blue color and there's a rock precipice behind. From the hotel a quarter of a mile above, people can look down and watch you fly."

○ *Marina Green, San Francisco, CA*
Michael McFadden, owner of the Kitemakers of San Francisco: "The Green is a good, flat,

grassy field with consistent westerly winds from 10 to 25 miles per hour. There's lots of parking. It's a beautiful place to fly, with the Golden Gate Bridge, Alcatraz, and Fort Mason in the distance, a yacht club beside the field, and handsome San Francisco Edwardian houses on the other side. There's other athletic activity at the field—joggers going by, volleyball games. In the summer when the San Joaquin Valley is over 100 degrees, ocean air is sucked through the Golden Gate and the field gets terrific, cool flying winds you can set your watch by. They come in right at three p.m. Usually the famous San Francisco fog comes in, too."

○ *Mission Bay, San Diego, CA*

Don Tabor, organizer of Top of the Line team: "The wind is almost *too* good and steady. We have to go to other places to practice for the erratic winds that we often encounter in tournaments around the country."

○ *San Ramon Mountain, CA*

Ron Romero, Sr., kite retailer and tournament organizer: "I walk 150 feet to the hill behind my house and from there I can fly. The mountain overlooks the town of San Ramon. The scenery is beautiful and tranquil, with Mount Diablo just ten miles away. From March through October, the wind blows like clockwork every day from noon until six o'clock. It does get hot many days—more

than 100 degrees. But this is okay because there's the breeze."

○ *The Lewis–Palmer Elementary School playground in Monument, CO*

Scott Skinner, kite enthusiast: "This is close to where I live. There are no other fliers, and it's nice and windy. The 7,200-foot altitude doesn't seem to have much effect on the flying. Since it's dry, the kites stay stiff and perform well. The air is a bit turbulent though, because of all the mountains. It's beautiful, with Pike's Peak in the background—the scenery people come to Colorado to see."

○ *Anastasia Park, St. Augustine, FL*

Mark Glick, founder of the Gator Kiters: "I fly right at The Cut, a gap between two islands, where the winds blow inland nice and cool all year-around. There are a lot of wind surfers there, so you know it's good for kites, too. The beach is hard-packed sand, and you can drive your car on it. It's convenient. You can fly right beside your car."

○ *South Ponte Vedra Beach, Jacksonville, FL*

Lisa Girolamo, of Kite Riggers: "It's a long beach with consistent wind, sand dunes, and a screen of mangrove trees. The wind always picks up sharply right at four in the afternoon and goes until dark. There aren't many people using it. I fly in my bathing suit year-around."

○ *National Seashore Park, Assateague Island, MD*

Billy Jones, expert East Coast flier: "It's a barrier island, about 40 miles long. There are no trees, just brush, so no matter what direction the wind is blowing, you can fly there. You fly on top of the dune and you fly like crazy. It's got solitude, and the winds are fantastic."

○ *Jockey's Ridge at Nags Head, NC*

Bill Baker of Peter Powell Kites: "It's an immense sand dune with a glorious view and wonderful historical associations to the Wright brothers."

○ *Field Six at Jones Beach State Park, Long Island, NY*

Robbi Sugarman, innovative New York Circus team flier: "There is wind there 11 months of the year, every month except August. August is flukey. For seven months the wind is between 15 and 30 miles an hour. And there's lots of room."

○ *Sunset Point, Erie, PA*

Sue Taft, national champion flier: "You can drive right to the beach. There are good steady winds, anything from southwest to northeast, coming right off Lake Erie. It's pretty. Sunsets out over the lake are spectacular. It's home—that's why it's the best place to fly for me."

○ *Brenton's Point, Newport, RI*

Margo Brown, past president of the American Kitefliers Association: "An elegant field with great wind. You can see the ships coming in; Europe is on the other side of the horizon. It's a marvelous 'soul' place to fly. My kite is my ship of the air. My imagination takes wing at Brenton's Point."

○ *The Peninsula, Long Beach, WA*

Bevan Brown (husband of Margo Brown), former American Kitefliers Association president: "It's a big, beautiful, 22-mile-long beach, often with unpredictable winds. You can't rest on your laurels there.

"You're challenged."

○ *McKinley Marina, Milwaukee, WI*

Randy Schmidt, co-owner of Striker Kites: "We have super flying there. It's a large peninsular landfill built into Lake Michigan. There are very few trees, so you get four winds, and no matter where it comes from it's good wind. Milwaukee is rated as the eighth-windiest city in the United States, so it's hard to get a bad day."

○*Signal Hill, St. John's, Newfoundland, Canada*

Skye Morrison, kite designer from Toronto: "I love to fly my stunter on the spot where Marconi launched a kite to send the first radio signal across the Atlantic to England. Marconi had to use a kite so he could get his wireless apparatus high enough to get the signal into the atmosphere. I love the historical association."

Festivals of the Air

Kite festivals are held all across the country on almost a year-round basis. Single-line festivals are adding more stunt kite components, and more fly-ins devoted exclusively to stunting are being scheduled.

You can obtain information on kite festivals in your area from the American Kitefliers Association, kite quarterlies, and newsletters (see listings elsewhere in this section), kite shops, and from stunt flying enthusiasts.

This list of some of the major annual events in the United States will give you some idea of when and where festivals are held, and something of their flavor:

March

○ *Gulf Coast Stunt Kite Challenge* at Surfside Beach, TX. Contact Linda Crumpler, Windwater Kites, 409/265–0868.

○ *International Kite Festival* at Rancho San Rafael, Reno, NV. Organized by kite expert Leland Toy. Contact Reno Visitors Authority, 702/827–7636.

○ *Oahu Kite Flying Festival* at Kapiolani Park, just outside Waikiki. Contact Tommy Kono, Parks and Recreation Department, 650 South King Street, Honolulu, HI 96813.

○ *Smithsonian Kite Festival* on the Washington Monument grounds. A rite of spring for many people. Contact Smithsonian Public Affairs Office, 1100 Jefferson Drive S.W., Washington, DC 20560. 202/357–4090.

April

○ *Maryland Kite Festival*. Location varies. A well-respected fly-in with a close link to *Kite Lines* magazine. Contact Mel Govig, 301/484–6287.

May

○ *East Coast Stunt Kite Championship* on the beach—the beach is so long it is called "The Sahara"—at Wildwood, NJ. Preregistration and fee. Contact Fran Gramkowski, High Fly Kite Company, 30 West End Avenue, Haddonfield, NJ 08033.

June

○ *Regional West Coast Stunt Kite Championship* at Marina Green, San Francisco, CA.

A lovely in-town field with good winds and great scenery. Contact Michael McFadden, Kitemakers of San Francisco, 590 Chestnut Street, San Francisco, CA 94133.

o *Rogallo Kite Festival* at Jockey's Ridge in Nags Head, NC. Honoring Francis Rogallo, inventor of the flexikite and flexible hang glider. Contact Kitty Hawk Kites, P.O. Box 340, Nags Head, NC 27959.

o *Summer Games Kite Contest* on the beach at Sands Ocean Club Resort Hotel, Myrtle Beach, SC. Contact Rick Kligman, Klig's Kites, 9600 North Kings Highway, Myrtle Beach, SC 29577.

o *Tail Grab Stunt Kite Contest* at East Mission Bay Park, San Diego, CA. The American version of Oriental fighter-kite duels. Registration fee, prizes. Contact John Perusse, Action Kites, 6284 Via Regla, San Diego, CA 92122.

July

o *Berkeley Marina Stunt Kite Competition* at North Waterfront Park, Berkeley, CA. Preregistration and fee. Contact Patty Donald–Poock, Recreation Department, 2180 Milvia Street, Berkeley, CA 94704.

o *Kite Festival International* at Brenton Point Park in Newport, RI An elegant site beside the ocean in one of America's most beautiful communities. Contact Tom Casselman, 365 Riverside Street, Portsmouth, RI 02871.

o *North Coast Stunt Kite Games*, Toledo, OH. Contact Al Hargus III, 4705 West Byron Street, Chicago, IL 60641.

August

o *Hawaii Kitefliers Association Festival* at Kapiolani Park, Honolulu. Contact Robert Loera, Kite Fantasy, 2863 Kalakaua Avenue, Honolulu, HI 96815.

o *Washington State International Kite Festival,* Long Beach, WA. One of the finest places to fly on the West Coast. Contact Washington State International Kite Festival, P.O. Box 797, Long Beach, WA 98631.

September

o *International Kite Festival* at D River Wayside, Lincoln City, OR. Contact Steve Lamb, Catch the Wind, 266 Southeast Highway 101, Lincoln City, OR 97367.

o *Stunt Kite Festival* at Jockey's Ridge, Nags

Head, NC. Contact Kitty Hawk Kites, P.O. Box 340, Nags Head, NC 27959. 919/441–4124.

○ *Sunfest Kite Festival* on the beach at 5th Street in Ocean City, MD. Flying beside the boardwalk means thousands of spectators. Lots of hospitality by sponsors. Cash prizes. Contact Bill Ochse, The Kite Loft (three locations in Ocean City), P.O. Box 551, Ocean City, MD 21842.

○ *West Coast Stunt Kite Championship* at Marina Green, San Francisco, CA. A major fly-in with cash prizes. Contact Michael McFadden, Kitemakers of San Francisco,

590 Chestnut Street, San Francisco, CA 94133.

October

○ *National Kite Championship.* Location varies. Held in conjunction with annual conference of American Kitefliers Association. Contact the AKA at 1559 Rockville Pike, Rockville, MD 20852.

○ *Ocean Shores Stunt Kite Competition* at Ocean Shores, WA. Contact Ocean Shores Kites, P.O. Box 607, Ocean Shores, WA 98569.

Anatomy of a Stunt Kite

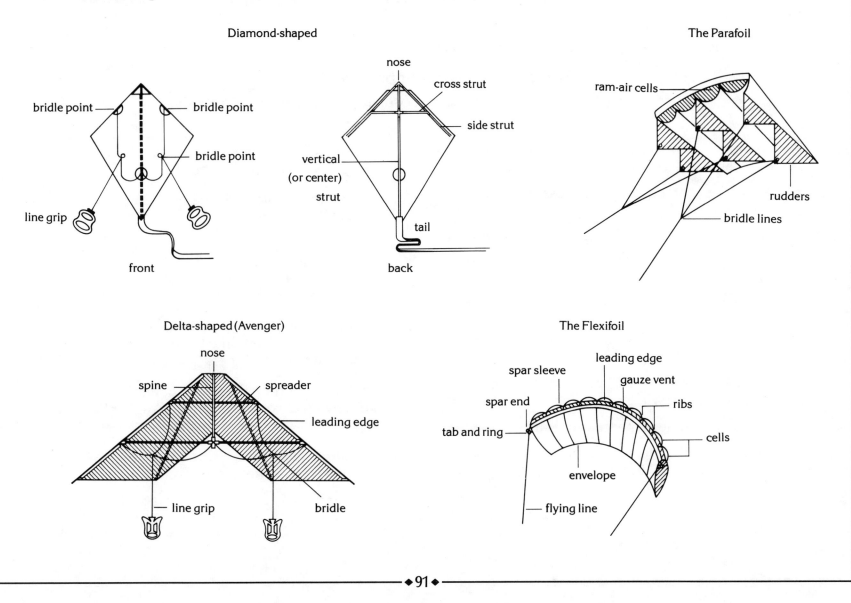

Diamond-shaped

bridle point

bridle point

bridle point

line grip

front

nose

cross strut

side strut

vertical
(or center)
strut

tail

back

The Parafoil

ram-air cells

rudders

bridle lines

Delta-shaped (Avenger)

nose

spine

spreader

leading edge

line grip

bridle

The Flexifoil

spar sleeve

leading edge

gauze vent

spar end

ribs

tab and ring

cells

envelope

flying line

Glossary

Talking Like a Pro

Stunt kiting has developed a lexicon of
words and phrases that fliers use to communicate among themselves.

big wings   large delta stunters, such as the Hawaiian Team Kite

carving   sweeping turns and cross-the-sky maneuvers

dog staking   looping the kite lines through a dog stake tether so the kite doubles back and performs close to flier

the edge   the point at which the kite stops moving forward

edgework   flying at the edge (the limit of the kite's ability to point into the wind)

fighter kite   a small, tailless, quick kite first flown in aerial duels in ancient Asia.

flair   a turn done at the stalling point at the edge

flipover   stalling the kite downwind and rotating the sail around its spar

fly the wind   standing your ground; trying not to move despite the pull of the kite

locking in   when a stack of kites locks into its correct flying formation

pilot   a stunt kite flier

power zone   the area of the sky where the kite's pulling power is greatest

powerflying   using a heavy-pulling kite to achieve human leaps into the air upward and forward; not for beginners

short-sticking   cutting the length of line used for stunt flying to compensate for a smaller flying area

slingshotting   an abrupt dive and sharp tug by a kite that was overhead and exerting no pull *solo artist*   a stunt flier who develops a completely individualistic style

stacks, trains   kites linked closely by lines and flown as a unit to achieve visual spectacle and greater power

strafe   a low-level ground pass

stunt flier's wrist   an inflammation of the wrist tendons resulting from the continual pull from a kite

tacho kichi   Japanese term for someone who is kite-crazy

tipwork   touching the wing-tip to the ground; also dragging it, or using it to hit a target

top gun   a real expert

upwind   toward or against the wind

whammer   a flier who favors very strong winds

whamming   sharp, abrupt maneuvers, often done close to the ground

wind window   the flying zone downwind of the flier and between the points where the wind pull tapers off (about nine o'clock on the left and three o'clock on the right)

The Right Kite

It's important to find a kite that suits your flying skill and local wind conditions as well as your wallet. This chart lists more than 80 dual-line kites currently available at kite and hobby stores, and through mail order companies. (For more information on mail order, see pages 82–83.)

This chart has categories for delta and diamond-shaped kites, with a separate section for other designs.

First, find your skill level: Beginner (never flew a stunt kite), Intermediate (some flying experience), or Advanced (several hours of flying with various kinds of stunt kites, in many wind conditions). Kites that can be flown with a range of experience are listed in both the Beginner to Advanced category and the Intermediate to Advanced category.

The estimated price of a stunt kite is the suggested retail cost: an inexpensive kite costs from $15 to $50; a moderate kite sells for $50 to $100; and a premium model is priced at more than $100.

Materials are listed for the kite sail (fabric areas) and the skeletal or frame area. (Example: ripstop nylon sail/fiberglass spars.)

The recommended line indicates whether line is included with the kite, or the test strength of line recommended by the manufacturer. (Example: 150 to 240-lb. test strength.)

The estimated wind range provided by the manufacturer indicates the wind conditions under which the kite performs best.

Deltas—Beginner

Stunt Kite	Manufacturer	Estimated Price	Size	Materials	Recommended Line (# means pound)	Estimated Wind Range
Aerobat	Skynasaur	inexpensive	52"×37"	ripstop nylon/ fiberglass spars	included	5–30 mph
Add-on kit	Skynasaur	inexpensive	52"×37"		included	5–30 mph
Aerobat Rainbow	Skynasaur	inexpensive	52"×37"	ripstop nylon/fiberglass spars	included	5–30 mph
Aerobat PL	Skynasaur	inexpensive	52"×37"	polyester laminate/ fiberglass spars	included	5–30 mph
Skyfox Single	Skynasaur	inexpensive	26"×18"	ripstop nylon/ fiberglass spars	included	6–40 mph
3-Train (Hot Train)	Skynasaur	moderate	26"×18"		included	6–40 mph
6-Train (Rainbow Train)	Skynasaur	premium	26"×18"		included	6–40 mph
Blazer	Striker Kites	inexpensive	66"×18"	ripstop nylon/fiberglass spars	included	5–25 mph
Aerosport	Striker Kites	premium	78"×30"	ripstop nylon/fiberglass spars	150–240# test line	8–30 mph
Stuntmaster	Dyna-Kite Corp.	inexpensive	44"×36"	ripstop nylon/ birchwood dowels	included	6–18 mph
Add-on kit	Dyna-Kite Corp.	inexpensive	44"×36"		included	6–18 mph
Flightmaster	Dyna-Kite Corp.	inexpensive	35"×29"	ripstop nylon/ birchwood dowels	included	6–25 mph
Add-on kit	Dyna-Kite Corp.	inexpensive	35"×29"		included	6–25 mph
Invisible	Renegade Kite Co.	moderate	72"×35"	clear Mylar/Kevlar skin w/poly grid fiberglass	50–110# test line	2–40 mph

Deltas—Beginner to Intermediate

Stunt Kite	Manufacturer	Estimated Price	Size	Materials	Recommended Line (# means pound)	Estimated Wind Range
Avenger	Avenger Kites	moderate	55″×35″	ripstop nylon/ fiberglass spars	100# test line	8–30 mph
Super Squirrel	Above It All Kites					
Single (7-panel)		moderate	77″×44″	ripstop nylon	100# test line	2–35 mph
Single (11-panel)		premium	77″×44″	ripstop nylon	100# test line	2–35 mph
Stars and Stripes		premium	77″×44″	ripstop nylon	100# test line	2–35 mph
Lightening Bolt		premium	77″×44″	ripstop nylon	100# test line	2–35 mph
Red Baron		premium	77″×44″	ripstop nylon	100# test line	2–35 mph
Art Deco		premium	77″×44″	ripstop nylon	100# test line	2–35 mph
HP		premium	77″×44″	ripstop nylon	100# test line	2–35 mph
Flame (custom design, contact dealers)		(ask)	77″×44″	ripstop nylon	100# test line	2–35 mph
Rainbow 3-Train	Skynasaur	moderate	36″×36″	ripstop nylon/fiberglass	included	5–30 mph

Deltas—Intermediate

Stunt Kite	Manufacturer	Estimated Price	Size	Materials	Recommended Line (# means pound)	Estimated Wind Range
Progressive Train Set of Aerobat, Skyfox, F36 (see Deltas—Beginner)	Skynasaur	moderate			included	5–30 mph
SW48	Skynasaur	inexpensive	48″×24″	ripstop nylon/ fiberglass spars	included	5–40 mph
C74 PL	Skynasaur	moderate	74″×49″	polyester laminate/ fiberglass spars	200# test line	5–40 mph
C74 Two-Color	Skynasaur	moderate	74″×49″	ripstop nylon/ fiberglass spars	200# test line	5–40 mph
C74 Rainbow	Skynasaur	moderate	74″×49″	ripstop nylon/ fiberglass spars	200# test line	5–40 mph
Lightfoot	Renegade Kite Co.	moderate	72″×35″	ripstop nylon/ fiberglass spars	50–100# test line	1–3 mph to 40 mph
Trainmaster 2-Train 3-Train	Dyna-Kite Corp.	inexpensive inexpensive	26″×23″ 26″×23″	ripstop nylon/ birchwood dowels	included included	7–20 mph 7–20 mph
The Graduate train of Trainmaster Flightmaster Stuntmaster	Dyna-Kite Corp.	moderate	26″×23″ 35″×29″ 44″×36″	ripstop nylon/ birchwood dowels	included	7–20 mph
The Raven	Crystal Kite Co.	premium	96″×48″	ripstop nylon/ fiberglass spars	200# test line	5–30 mph
Freebird	Crystal Kite Co.	premium	96″×48″	ripstop nylon/ fiberglass spars	200# test line	5–30 mph

Deltas—intermediate, continued

Stunt Kite	Manufacturer	Estimated Price	Size	Materials	Recommended Line (# means pound)	Estimated Wind Range
A-Roar-A2200	Go Fly a Kite	moderate	86″×29″	ripstop nylon/ fiberglass spars	100–200# test line	5–30 mph
Star Fighter						
3-Train	Hyperkites	inexpensive	18″×11″	ripstop nylon/ hardwood birch dowels	included	10–40 mph
6-Train	Hyperkites	moderate	18″×11″		included	10–40 mph
9-Train	Hyperkites	moderate	18″×11″		included	10–40 mph
Star Cruiser						
Single	Hyperkites	inexpensive	28″×16″	ripstop nylon/ hardwood birch dowels	included	7–40 mph
2-Train	Hyperkites	inexpensive	28″×16″		included	7–40 mph
3-Train	Hyperkites	moderate	28″×16″		included	7–40 mph
4-Train	Hyperkites	moderate	28″×16″		included	7–40 mph
6-Train	Hyperkites	moderate	28″×16″		included	7–40 mph
8-Train	Hyperkites	premium	28″×16″		included	7–40 mph
Add-on	Hyperkites	inexpensive	28″×16″		not included	7–40 mph
Star Master	Hyperkites	moderate	42″×21″	ripstop nylon/hardwood birch dowels	included	4–40 mph
Add-on	Hyperkites	inexpensive	42″×21″		included	4–40 mph
Spyro-Jet	L'Atelier duVent	premium	88″×30″	ripstop nylon/ fiberglass spars	150–200# test line	8–40 mph
Ultralight Spyro-Jet	L'Atelier duVent	premium	79″×28″	ripstop nylon/ fiberglass spars	100# test line	4–40 mph
Revenger	Avenger Kites	moderate	60″×35″	ripstop nylon/ fiberglass spars	100# test line	5–25 mph
Mustang	Dan Wheeler Kites	moderate	80″×25″	ripstop nylon/fiberglass spars	150# test line	5–25 mph

Deltas—Intermediate to Advanced

Stunt Kite	Manufacturer	Estimated Price	Size	Materials	Recommended Line (# means pound)	Estimated Wind Range
Renegade I (solid color)	Renegade Kite Co.	moderate	72"×35"	ripstop nylon/graphite	120–200# test line	3–40 mph
Renegade II (2-color appliqué)	Renegade Kite Co.	moderate	72"×35"	ripstop nylon/graphite	120–200# test line	3–40 mph
Renegade III (predesigned appliqué choice of colors)	Renegade Kite Co.	premium	72"×35"	ripstop nylon/graphite	120–200# test line	3–40 mph
Hawaiian Team Kite	Top of the Line Kites	premium	96"×45"	ripstop nylon/ fiberglass spars	150–300# test line	4–40 mph
Spin Off Team Kite	Top of the Line Kites	premium	96"×45"	ripstop nylon/ fiberglass spars	100# test line	4–40 mph
Ultralight Spin Off	Top of the Line Kites	premium	96"×45"	ripstop nylon/ graphite spars	100# test line	4–40 mph

Deltas—Advanced

Stunt Kite	Manufacturer	Estimated Price	Size	Materials	Recommended Line (# means pound)	Estimated Wind Range
Challenger Delta	Striker Kites	premium	114"×30"	ripstop nylon/ fiberglass spars	135–200# test line	8–35 mph
Force 10 Delta	Striker Kites	premium	180"×54"	ripstop nylon/ fiberglass spars	500# test line	6–25 mph
8-Foot Delta Wing	Peter Powell Kites	premium	96"×36"	ripstop nylon/ fiberglass spars	200# test line	7–40 mph

Diamond-shaped—Beginner

Stunt Kite	Manufacturer	Estimated Price	Size	Materials	Recommended Line (# means pound)	Estimated Wind Range
Trlby single	Trlby Products	inexpensive	36"×36"	polyethylene/fiberglass	included	5–20 mph
2-pack	Trlby Products	inexpensive	36"×36"	polyethylene/fiberglass	included	5–20 mph
3-pack	Trlby Products	inexpensive	36"×36"	polyethylene/fiberglass	included	5–20 mph
6-pack	Trlby Products	moderate	36"×36"	polyethylene/fiberglass	included	5–20 mph
Add-on kit	Trlby Products	inexpensive	36"×36"	polyethylene/fiberglass	included	5–20 mph
Trlby Ripstop (solid color)				ripstop nylon/fiberglass		
Single	Trlby Products	inexpensive	36"×36"		included	5–20 mph
Triple	Trlby Products	moderate	36"×36"		included	5–20 mph
Add-on kit	Trlby Products	inexpensive	36"×36"		included	5–20 mph
Trlby Ripstop (striped)				ripstop nylon/fiberglass		
Single	Trlby Products	inexpensive	36"×36"		included	5–20 mph
Triple	Trlby Products	moderate	36"×36"		included	5–20 mph
Add-on kit	Trlby Products	inexpensive	36"×36"		included	5–20 mph
Squirrel				ripstop nylon/fiberglass	20–30# test line	
Single	Above it All Kites	inexpensive	48"×22"			4–35 mph
3-Train		moderate	48"×22"			4–35 mph
Tempest				ripstop nylon/fiberglass	50–75# test line	
Single solid	Above it All Kites	inexpensive	55"×28"			4–35 mph
Diamond		moderate	55"×28"			4–35 mph
3-pack		premium	55"×28"			4–35 mph

Diamond-shaped—Beginner, continued

Stunt Kite	Manufacturer	Estimated Price	Size	Materials	Recommended Line (# means pound)	Estimated Wind Range
4 Foot Poly- ethylene	Peter Powell Kites	inexpensive	48″×48″	polyethylene/fiberglass	included	10 mph
Add-on kit	Peter Powell Kites	inexpensive	48″×48″	polyethylene/fiberglass	included	10 mph
3-Train	Peter Powell Kites	moderate	48″×48″	polyethylene/fiberglass/ linked ready to fly	included	10 mph
6-Train	Peter Powell Kites	premium	48″×48″	polyethylene/fiberglass/ linked ready to fly	included	10 mph
4 Foot Ripstop	Peter Powell Kites	inexpensive	48″×48″	ripstop nylon/fiberglass	included	10 mph
Add-on kit	Peter Powell Kites	inexpensive	48″×48″	ripstop nylon/fiberglass	included	10 mph
3-Train	Peter Powell Kites	premium	48″×48″	ripstop nylon/fiberglass/ linked ready to fly	included	10 mph
6-Train	Peter Powell Kites	premium	48″×48″	ripstop nylon/fiberglass/ linked ready to fly	included	10 mph
4 Foot Tricolor Ripstop	Peter Powell Kites	inexpensive	48″×48″	ripstop nylon/fiberglass	included	10 mph
Add-on kit	Peter Powell Kites	inexpensive	48″×48″	ripstop nylon/fiberglass	included	10 mph
3-Train	Peter Powell Kites	premium	48″×48″	ripstop nylon/fiberglass	included	10 mph
6-Train	Peter Powell Kites	premium	48″×48″	ripstop nylon/fiberglass	included	10 mph
Aero Stunter	Go Fly a Kite	inexpensive	36″×36″	ripstop nylon/fiberglass	included	3 mph
3-Train	Go Fly a Kite	moderate	36″×36″	ripstop nylon/fiberglass	included	3 mph
6-Train	Go Fly a Kite	premium	36″×36″	ripstop nylon/fiberglass	included	3 mph
Black Widow	Go Fly a Kite	inexpensive	36″×36″	ripstop nylon/fiberglass	included	3 mph
3-Train	Go Fly a Kite	inexpensive	36″×36″	ripstop nylon/fiberglass	included	3 mph
6-Train	Go Fly a Kite	moderate	36″×36″	ripstop nylon/fiberglass	included	3 mph
F+1 Stunter	Frontier Kites	inexpensive	48″×48″	ripstop nylon/fiberglass	included	5 mph
Add-on kit	Frontier Kites	inexpensive	48″×48″	ripstop nylon/fiberglass	included	5 mph
3-Train	Frontier Kites	moderate	48″×48″	ripstop nylon/fiberglass	included	5 mph
5-Train	Frontier Kites	premium	48″×48″	ripstop nylon/fiberglass	included	5 mph
F36	Skynasaur Kites	inexpensive	36″×36″	ripstop nylon/fiberglass	included	5–30 mph
Add-on kit	Skynasaur Kites	inexpensive	36″×36″	ripstop nylon/fiberglass	included	5–30 mph
Rainbow	Skynasaur Kites	inexpensive	36″×36″	ripstop nylon/fiberglass	included	5–30 mph
3-Train	Skynasaur Kites	moderate	36″×36″	ripstop nylon/fiberglass	included	5–30 mph

Diamond-shaped—Intermediate

Stunt Kite	Manufacturer	Estimated Price	Size	Materials	Recommended Line (# means pound)	Estimated Wind Range
4-Foot Mark II Triple Bridled	Peter Powell Kites	moderate	48"×48"	ripstop nylon/ without tail	included	10 mph
6-Foot Ripstop Nylon	Peter Powell Kites	premium	72"×72"	ripstop nylon/ graphite rods	200# test line	5 mph
The Caution Kite	Crystal Kites	moderate	34"×34"	ripstop nylon/fiberglass	50–100# test line	7 mph

Unique Shapes—Beginner

Stunt Kite	Manufacturer	Estimated Price	Size	Materials	Recommended Line (# means pound)	Estimated Wind Range
Ghosts Set	Hyperkites	moderate	21"×42"	ripstop nylon/fiberglass	included	3–10 mph
F-16 Fighting Falcon (limited ed.)	Sky Delights	premium	45"×51"	ripstop nylon/fiberglass/ hardwood spars	50# test line	3–20 mph
The Zeta Wing	Don Gellert Kites	moderate	51"×35"	ripstop nylon/fiberglass/ hardwood spars	50# test line	3–20 mph

Unique Shapes—Beginner to Intermediate

Stunt Kite	Manufacturer	Estimated Price	Size	Materials	Recommended Line (# means pound)	Estimated Wind Range
Stacker	Flexifoil International	premium	72" wing-span	ripstop nylon/ fiberglass spars	50–100# test line	8–40 mph
w/control bar	Flexifoil International	premium				
Skycycle (stunt rotor kite)	Skycycle Kites	inexpensive	21" long	formed from rigid laminated styrene w/hardwood axle	included	5+ mph
Flexifoil	Flexifoil International	moderate	48" wing-span	ripstop nylon/fiberglass	50# test line	12–40 mph
Hot Shot 4	Flexifoil International	moderate	48" wing-span	ripstop nylon/fiberglass	50# test line	12–40 mph

Unique Shapes—Intermediate

Stunt Kite	Manufacturer	Estimated Price	Size	Materials	Recommended Line (# means pound)	Estimated Wind Range
Flexifoil	Flexifoil International	moderate	48" wing-span	ripstop nylon/fiberglass	50# test line	12–40 mph
Hot Shot 4	Flexifoil International	moderate	48" wing-span	ripstop nylon/fiberglass	50# test line	12–40 mph
Stacker	Flexifoil International	premium	72" wing-span	ripstop nylon	50–100# test line	8–40 mph
Stacker w/control bar	Flexifoil International	premium	72" wing-span	ripstop nylon/fiberglass	50–100# test line	8–40 mph
Rainbow	Flexifoil International	premium	72" wing-span	ripstop nylon/fiberglass	50–100# test line	8–40 mph
Rainbow w/control bar	Flexifoil International	premium	72" wing-span	ripstop nylon/fiberglass	50–100# test line	8–40 mph
Custom	Flexifoil International	premium	72" wing-span	ripstop nylon/fiberglass	50–100# test line	8–40 mph

Unique Shapes—Intermediate to Advanced

Stunt Kite	Manufacturer	Estimated Price	Size	Materials	Recommended Line (# means pound)	Estimated Wind Range
Super 10	Flexifoil International	premium	120" wing-span	ripstop nylon/fiberglass	100–200# test line	7–40 mph
w/control bar and line	Flexifoil International	premium	120" wing-span	ripstop nylon/fiberglass	included	7–40 mph
Rainbow	Flexifoil International	premium	120" wing-span	ripstop nylon/fiberglass	100–200# test line	7–40 mph
Rainbow w/control bar and line	Flexifoil International	premium	120" wing-span	ripstop nylon/fiberglass	included	7–40 mph
Custom Rainbow	Flexifoil International	premium	72" wing-span	ripstop nylon/fiberglass	100–200# test line	7–40 mph
Hyper 16	Flexifoil International	premium	192" wing-span	ripstop nylon/fiberglass	100–200# test line	7–20 mph
Revolution I	Neos Omega	premium	108"×36"	ripstop nylon/high-modular graphite	200# test line	3–40 mph

Index

About the Authors

Ali Fujino has been fascinated by flight since her childhood, when she was raised as something of a tomboy by her baseball-playing father. After studying museum operations at the Smithsonian Institution, she was a consultant to museums all over the world for more than ten years. In 1981, she qualified as the only woman member of the United States Boomerang team which successfully challenged Australia. She now operates her own design and production firm in Seattle.

Ben Ruhe has a lifelong interest in kites and other flying objects. A founder of the United States Boomerang Association, he was captain of the U.S. boomerang team that defeated Australia in 1981. He is presently an honorary consultant on boomerangs to the Smithsonian's National Air and Space Museum, and a consultant to art galleries in Washington, D.C. His other books include *Boomerang: How to Make, Throw, and Catch It,* with Eric Darnell (1985), and *Many Happy Returns* (1977).